PRIVATES
ON PARADE

by the same author

A DAY IN THE DEATH OF JOE EGG
THE NATIONAL HEALTH or Nurse Norton's Affair
FORGET-ME-NOT LANE
CHEZ NOUS: A Domestic Comedy in Two Acts
THE FREEWAY

PRIVATES ON PARADE

A Play with Songs
in Two Acts by

PETER NICHOLS

FABER & FABER
3 Queen Square
London

First published in 1977
by Faber and Faber Limited
3 Queen Square London WC1
Printed in Great Britain by
Latimer Trend & Company Ltd Plymouth
All rights reserved

© 1977 by Peter Nichols

British Library Cataloguing in Publication Data

Nichols, Peter, b. 1927
    Privates on parade.
    I. Title
    822'.9'14   PR6064.12P/
    ISBN 0-571-11142-4

To THELMA

Characters

MAJOR GILES FLACK, aged 55
ACTING CAPTAIN TERRI DENNIS, aged 45
SERGEANT MAJOR REG DRUMMOND, aged 35
SYLVIA MORGAN, aged 28
FLIGHT SERGEANT KEVIN CARTWRIGHT, aged 22
CORPORAL LEN BONNY, aged 35
LANCE CORPORAL CHARLES BISHOP, aged 20
LEADING AIRCRAFTMAN ERIC YOUNG-LOVE, aged 20
PRIVATE STEVEN FLOWERS, aged 20
LEE ⎱ non-speaking Chinese
CHENG ⎰

Privates on Parade received its first performance at the Aldwych Theatre in February 1977. The cast was as follows:

LANCE CORPORAL CHARLES BISHOP	Tim Wylton
CORPORAL LEN BONNY	Joe Melia
FLIGHT SERGEANT KEVIN CARTWRIGHT	Ben Cross
CHENG	John Venning
ACTING CAPTAIN TERRI DENNIS	Denis Quilley
SERGEANT MAJOR REG DRUMMOND	David Daker
MAJOR GILES FLACK	Nigel Hawthorne
PRIVATE STEVEN FLOWERS	Ian Gelder
LEE	Richard Rees
SYLVIA MORGAN	Emma Williams
LEADING AIRCRAFTMAN ERIC YOUNG-LOVE	Simon Jones

Directed by Michael Blakemore
Designed by Michael Annals
Choreography by Eleanor Fazan
Music by Denis King

The sets more or less alternate front-cloth and full-stage, in the manner of the variety theatre. Lee and Cheng sometimes move furniture and props, to the accompaniment of percussion, thus suggesting the popular Chinese opera.

Over the proscenium, downstage, is a sign-writing screen on which are flashed the names of the various scenes, given in the script. Steps provide easy access from stalls to stage and musicians are unseen in a pit.

A front-cloth is down as audience arrives.

ACT ONE

SCENE ONE
The Quartermaster's Stores

The front-cloth shows a jungle design with the play's title.
Lights go down and out and cloth flies. Bare stage, and no lights for some time. At last someone strikes a match upstage and comes down by its light.
We see STEVEN FLOWERS, *in khaki drill and beret, shouldering kit-bag with bush-hat strung to it. Match burns low and he blows it out. He drops kit-bag on floor, waits again, wipes face with handkerchief.*

STEVE: Anyone home?
    (*Pause. No answer.*)
    Hullo?
    (*Waits again. Shrugs, takes piece of paper from tunic pocket, looks at it. Picks up kit-bag again and makes to go. As he disappears an overhead light is switched on, showing a narrow circle of stage floor.* LEN BONNY *comes from side, pushing a skip. Dressed as* STEVE *but with three stripes. On skip is clipboard with papers.* LEN *is by turns aggressive and morose, with a Midlands accent.* STEVE *comes back into the light.* LEN *jumps.*)
LEN: Where d'you fucking come from?
STEVE: Bukit Timah, Sarge. Up the Bukit Timah Road.
LEN: I don't mean where d'you fucking come from in Singapore? I mean what you doing creeping in here like a fucking mouse?
STEVE: Come to get my arrival chitty cleared.
    (LEN *takes* STEVE'*s chit, looks at it with some suspicion, forms words with his lips.*)
LEN: Private Flowers.

(LEN *looks at* STEVE *as if to verify this. He sees a twenty-year-old, untouched, suntanned conscript who speaks with a West Country accent.*)

Clerk special duties. In . . . tell . . .

STEVE: Intelligence.

(LEN *looks at him again.*)

LEN: I can fucking read! Intelligence, eh? You'll be all right here. It's all fucking long words here. A shower of fucking Einsteins here. Where d'you come from?

STEVE: Bukit Timah, Sarge. In a gharrie up the Bukit Timah Road.

LEN: Not in Singapore! In Blighty.

STEVE: Swindon.

LEN: Railway junction.

STEVE: That's it.

LEN: Railway town. D'you work on the railway?

STEVE: I came in straight from school. I'm going to be a teacher.

LEN: You'll be all right here. All la-di-dah round here. And fucking elocution. (*Looks at chit again.*) Demob Group Seventy-Three.

STEVE: Roll on the boat!

LEN: Not for you, not yet, sonny boy. You won't be getting no cunting boat for a good while yet.

STEVE: What's your demob group, Sarge?

LEN: You don't catch me with no group number. No fucking fear. Regular, me. Five-year tour. Three up, two to go. Right. Better get you cleared. (*Pushes off skip and turns on another light, pulls down a small shelf at side of stage, stands behind it. Puts chit on shelf and issues kit.*) Stripes, sergeants', khaki drill, pairs two. Everyone here gets three stripes up.

STEVE: You mean we're all sergeants? Just like that?

LEN: Temporary, acting, unpaid. Just so we can use the messes when we go away. And all the civvies got some pips up. So don't call me fucking sergeant. Only two of my stripes is substantive.

STEVE: Right you are, Corporal.

LEN: No, it's all fucking first names here. So you better call me Len and I'll call you fucking Einstein, all right?

(STEVE *has taken the stripes and is trying them against his sleeve.*)
Or I could call you Swindon. See how things turn out.
(LEN *ticks list on board, goes off.* STEVE *pins the stripes on, looks at them, smiles with pleasure.*)

STEVE: (*Quietly*) Dear Everyone at 56, as you see by the top of this letter form, from now on your errant son and heir is to be addressed as *Sergeant* Flowers. Which I take to be a long-overdue recognition of my innate genius.

LEN: (*Reappearing*) Badges, cap, pairs, one. Incorporating faces, pairs one, face to the left smiling, face to the right browned off.
(STEVE *looks at badges.*)

STEVE: They're the tragic and comic masks.

LEN: The what?

STEVE: The masks of tragedy and comedy.

LEN: Get out! Typical, that is. No cunt never tells me nothing. Stores-basher me, always have been, that's my trade, right? I know stocktaking, requisitioning, I know the regulation issue backwards. (*Fast.*) Boots, mosquito, jungle-green, soldier's.

STEVE: See what you mean, Len.

LEN: Comforters, cap, khaki, other ranks. All right, then all of a sudden I'm posted here and put to handling these cunts: shoes, black, patent, dancing, tap. Type Astaire, Fred. Pairs, one.
(LEN *gives shoes to* STEVE, *ticks list.* STEVE *stows in kit-bag.* LEN *produces cardboard box.*)
Sticks, greasepaint, assorted, six. Putty, nose, portions one. Eyes, shadow, jars one. Puffs, powder, other ranks, one. *And* I wasn't put on no course, I had to pick it all up. (*Points to side.*) But what about that section over there? How'm I supposed to inventory all that? Tights, fishnet, black, sergeant's. Male oblique female. Brassière sequinned, inflatable, sergeant's. Wigs, auburn, wavy, officers.
(LEN *has shown* STEVE *some of these.*)

STEVE: The lady officers?

LEN: The fucking men. Ain't enough tarts to go round so the

men get up in frocks.

STEVE: Do I get a frock?

LEN: Only against a proper requisition.

STEVE: I don't fancy wearing frocks.

LEN: *Nil desperandum.* It may never happen. You can come here as a concert fucking pianist and end up shovelling shit. Look at me—sparks, chippy, Jack-of-fucking-all-Trades. And I came in as an *accordionist*! (*Closes up shelf and moves centre, signing chit, which he gives to* STEVE.) You'll be attached to Captain Dennis. I'll take you along there now.

STEVE: (*Shouldering bag*) What's he like?

LEN: Terri? Easy-going. San Fairy Fucking Ann. You know, typical civvie.

TERRI: (*From back of theatre*) There you are, Leonora! At long last!

SCENE TWO
On with the Show

LEN: Hullo, Terri. We been waiting for *you.*

TERRI: Who's your friend?

LEN: Sergeant Flowers. He's going to be attached to your section.

TERRI: (*Arriving on stage from stalls*) It sounds heaven.
(TERRI *is suntanned, has dyed blond hair, plucked and pencilled eyebrows, matt tan base, wearing pastel-coloured slacks and shirt, smoking cigarette in holder. His voice is Shaftesbury Avenue pasted over Lancashire.*)
Sweetie, I can hardly wait to attach you to my section but we're supposed to be rehearsing and let's face it, we've wasted enough time——

LEN: We been waiting for *you.*

TERRI: You dare speak to an officer like that I'll scream the place down. Go to your post this instant! And you, duckie, I should drop that expensive looking handbag and find yourself somewhere to sit.

(STEVE *drops kit-bag on stage.*)

Not here, duckie, this is the stage. Those are the wings, that is the front-of-house, up there are the flies and the whole bag of tricks is known as The Theatre.

(LEN *leads the bewildered* STEVE *into the wings.*)

And now perhaps young Tom Edison will give us our opening lights. And is everyone ready backstage?

CHORUS: (*Off*) Yes, all ready, etc.

(*House lights up.*)

TERRI: It's fabulous!

(TERRI *goes off, immediately comes back acting. He's a stilted performer, always playing out front, even when speaking to someone on stage.*)

Great Heavens, look at this! Rehearsals due and no one here. I've never seen such amateurs. Dear oh Lord! Are *you* there, Sparks?

LEN: Yes, I'm here, Terri.

TERRI: Then give me your working lights.

(*Overhead light comes on.*)

And take out your house lights.

(*Blackout.*)

LEN: (*Off*) Fucking thing!

(*Working lights on again. In the blackout* KEVIN *has come on: good-looking, wearing sunglasses and white shirt, khaki shorts, etc. London accent, awkward actor.*)

KEVIN: Hullo, Terri——

TERRI: Ah! Someone's condescended to join me. (*To audience.*) Flight Sergeant Kevin Cartwright, RAF.

KEVIN: Sorry I wasn't here on time. I couldn't find my glasses. And one of them had a drink left in it.

TERRI: One of them had a drink—I find that totally outrageous!

(CHARLES *comes on, twenty but putting on weight and losing hair, camp but matronly, Yorkshire accent.*)

CHARLES: Sorry I wasn't here on time.

TERRI: Well, Sergeant Charles Bishop, Royal Army Medical Corps, what's your excuse?

CHARLES: You know how fond I am of music.

TERRI: Well?

CHARLES: I've been listening to a three-piece orchestra.

TERRI: Yes?

CHARLES: And the third piece was rather long.

TERRI: This is too much honestly! Take your places without another word.

(LEN *has come on. He cannot act at all.*)

LEN: Sorry I was not here on time.

TERRI: Never mind, Sergeant Len Bonny, Royal Electrical and Mechanical Engineers, tell me, where've you been?

LEN: I've been buying my wife a dress.

TERRI: A dress? That's nice. What kind of a dress?

LEN: A Biblical dress.

TERRI: A Biblical dress? What's that when it's at home?

LEN: You know—Low and Behold!

TERRI: (*With gestures to explain*) Low—and behold?

LEN: I shall find it hard to look her in the face.

TERRI: You'll find it hard to look—I refuse to listen to another solitary word.

(ERIC *has come on, plain, ungainly, hair shaved well above ears, wearing issue glasses and sweating profusely into KD. Has plummy voice and hearty demotic manner.*)

Who's this? Sergeant Eric Young-Love, RAF. You're late for rehearsal.

ERIC: I've been eating at my girl-friend's.

TERRI: Is your girl-friend a good cook?

ERIC: Oh Lord no! Even the mouse ite eat. Mice eat out!

TERRI: Oh, Jesus!

ERIC: I can do it, honestly, Terri——

TERRI: Even Leonora got her lines right.

LEN: And I didn't come here as an actor. I come as a fucking accordionist.

TERRI: All right! Carry on. (*Claps hands for attention.*) Well, everyone's here but Sylvia. Where is Sylvia, where is she? (*They all pretend to search the stage.* SYLVIA *appears centre: Eurasian, beautiful, speaks with Indian intonation, wears dress and high-heeled shoes.*)

SYLVIA: (*Joins them looking*) Who are we looking for?

TERRI: You! Temporary Lieutenant Sylvia Morgan of no fixed

abode. Where have you been?

SYLVIA: I'd rather you didn't say that, Terri.

TERRI: What—where've you been?

SYLVIA: Of no fixed abode. It doesn't sound very nice.

TERRI: It only means you're not in any of the services, duckie.

SYLVIA: I'm sorry but it makes me sound not entirely respectable.

TERRI: My dears, the temperament. You'd think it was Drury
   Lane. Get on!

SYLVIA: I've been answering an advert for a girl to help in the
   officers' mess.

TERRI: Did you get the job?

SYLVIA: No, they said they wanted a girl who'd been in a mess
   before.

TERRI: I will not countenance another word! Are you all ready?

CHORUS: Yes.

TERRI: Are you all steady?

CHORUS: Yes.

TERRI: Then lights, action, music!
   (*Stage lighting, they line up and band strikes up. They sing
   their opener.*)

CHORUS: What shall we do for an opening number?
   Waltzes are schmaltz and we're sick of the rhumba,
   Crests of the wave are too hackneyed by far.
   Hey, what about letting them know who we are?

   We're SADUSEA
   And on the other hand we're glad to see
   You've come along tonight to join our laughter,
   To see our dance,
   To feel a touch of magic and a breath of romance.
   We've taken pains
   To see our show's the sort that entertains
   And now there's nothing very much remaining
   Except for naming
   The company;
   We're SADUSEA,
   We're S.A.D.U.S.E.A.,
   Song and dance unit South East Asia.

(CHORUS *move about in planned confusion and take individual lines in the next verse.*)

    What can we do for the rest of the chorus?
    They know who we are so they know what to call us.
    We're ready and steady and rarin' to go.
    Hey, what about saying the name of the show?

(*Cloth comes down behind* CHORUS *as they again form line and sing in unison.*)

    It's Jamboree,
    We're bringing you a Jungle Jamboree.
    We've got together in this equatorial latitude,
    To chase your blues away and change your attitude.
    So now you'll see
    We've got the kind of personality
    To make you come with us upon a spree
    Or a pot-pourri
    Or a jubilee
    So one-two-three
    For S.A.D.U.S.E.A.
    And their jingle-jangle-jungle jamboree!
(CHORUS *dance off.*)

SCENE THREE
Single Men in Barracks

Cloth flown to reveal a bar counter with shelves of bottles behind, stools in front. LEE *and* CHENG *wearing black place other chairs and table downstage while Chinese percussion is played. After setting stage, they bow.* LEE *goes behind the bar.* CHENG *stands to one side.*

Enter REG DRUMMOND, *tough, good-looking, wearing* CSM's *insignia. He is followed by* STEVE, *still shouldering kit-bag.*

REG: This is the mess.

STEVE: Very nice.

REG: And I'm the mess steward. Any complaints, any problems, let me know. Any cheek from Lee. This is Lee. Number one boy. Sarnt Flowers, he belongee mess now.

(LEE, *polishing glasses, nods.*)

And this is Cheng, Cheng take Sergeant's kit to bearer, tell him fix velly good bed chop-chop, or my ask plenty questions. Savvy?

(CHENG *nods, takes bag from* STEVE, *goes.*)

Sit down, have a drink.

STEVE: Well, thanks, Sergeant Major, I'll have a ginger-beer shandy.

REG: Two large gins, Lee. Plenty big like-so.

(REG *and* STEVE *sit at a table while* LEE *prepares drinks.*)

You'd better get used to calling me Reg. Who else have you met so far?

STEVE: Sarnt Bonny gave me my kit, then——

REG: Poor old Len. Puggled.

STEVE: Is he?

REG: Doollaly.

STEVE: I thought he——

REG: Wouldn't *you* be round the bend if they'd posted you direct from Iceland to India? Straight from jackets fleece-lined to nets mosquito?

(REG *laughs. Drinks served.*)

Cheers.

STEVE: Cheers.

(REG *and* STEVE *drink.* STEVE *coughs on his.*)

Could I have some orange in it?

(LEE *pours some.*)

Then I saw Captain Dennis.

REG: What d'you make of Captain Dennis?

STEVE: He struck me as a bit of a pseudo-intellectual.

REG: *Did* he?

STEVE: A bit of an eccentric Bohemian, I thought.

REG: Not to mention a bum-boy.

STEVE: Is he?

REG: A raver.

STEVE: Is he a homo then? I'm not sure I've ever met any homos before, not to speak to.

REG: You will here. Queen's Own, this is. The Middlesex Regiment. And if you want my advice you'll give the bum-boys a wide berth. That is, if you don't want to be RTU'd.

STEVE: RTU'd?

REG: Returned to Unit. Major Flack doesn't like the bum-boys either. He doesn't want his brother-officers saying, 'Hullo there, Giles, how are those bum-boys of yours coming along?' He knows that many of the men under his command are young, hardy soldiers, entrusted to his care, he respects that trust, he won't have civilian perverts bringing in a lot of bum-boy expressions that your average squaddie wouldn't think of in a month of Sundays. Have another?

STEVE: I'd like to buy *you* one but till next pay-day I'm a bit——

REG: You can start running up a bill now you're a member. Two more, Lee, puttee book Sarnt Flowers. And if you get any trouble with any of them, funny business in the ablutions, admiring your John Thomas, any of that, have a word with me. Deal with them between us, eh?

STEVE: Right-oh, Sarnt Major.

REG: Reg.

STEVE: Reg.

REG: Deal with them the same way we used to in the Force.

STEVE: The force?

REG: The Metropolitan Police. Cheers. Same with the Chinese boys. Or your Indian bearer.

STEVE: Are they bum-boys as well then?

REG: Stealing I mean. Insubordination. Being late with the dhobi.
(LEE *serves two more gins.*)
I got a room on the perimeter, what I call my interrogation room. Haven't I, Lee? You've been there once, haven't you? They don't often go twice, do they, Lee? Tell him what it's like, go on.
(REG *sips gin while* LEE *pours orange into* STEVE'*s.*)
No windows, no furniture, an old guard-house. White-washed walls. I have them whitewashed periodically. I won't have uppity wogs on my patch. Will I, Lee?

STEVE: Cheers. (*Drinks as* LEE *returns to bar.*)

REG: You any use with a gun?

STEVE: I've used a sten on the range.

REG: Only I'm i/c dog-shooting. Not much other game on the
island but dog's all right from a jeep, they can give you a
fair old run.

STEVE: I'm quite fond of dogs actually. We've got an Aberdeen
Terrier at home. He's called Mac.

REG: I'm not talking about Scotties! These are poxy suppurating
curs. I won't have rabies on my manor.

STEVE: (*Presenting his arrival chit*) If you'll sign my arrival
chitty, I'll be getting on.

(REG *drinks.* STEVE *lays the chit on the table before him.* STEVE
finishes his gin, coughs, while REG *slowly looks at his form.
Then he sits up and studies* STEVE.)

REG: Intelligence.

STEVE: Attached to the service corps, yes.

REG: Criminal Investigation, by any chance?

STEVE: No, just routine security stuff. Trying to stop the stores
being nicked. D'you want my pen?

REG: No stores being nicked round here. No loose-wallahs in my
bailiwick.

(LEN *and* CHARLES *come on.* LEN *sits at table.*)

LEN: Fucking foot-rash. Itches to buggery.

CHARLES: Two Tigers, Lee, there's a sweetheart.

(CHARLES *removes* LEN'S *shoe and sock and examines his foot.*
CHENG *has returned, bringing case of drinks for bar.*)

Cheng, run and get that lotion on our bedside table.

(CHENG *goes, as* KEVIN *comes on.*)

LEN: D'you reckon it's tinea this or athlete's foot?

KEVIN: Tinea's what you get on your knackers.

LEN: I got it on my knackers and all. I'm fucking covered in
gentian violet.

KEVIN: (*Sings*) There's a blue ring round my balls
It's Tinea——

LEN: I thought what you got on your knackers was dhobi itch.

CHARLES: Never mind what it's called. Just remember to change
the dressing regularly and let the air get to it.

(CHENG *returns with bottle of lotion and* CHARLES *kneels and applies it to* LEN's *feet.* LEE *serves beers.*)

Wear chapplies whenever you can. What's the use me doing a Florence Nightingale if you don't follow instructions?

REG: I'm going. I can't watch this.

(REG *goes off. Unsteadily, lurching into* CHENG *who holds him up.* REG *wrenches away.* CHARLES *continues, kneeling before* LEN, *who drinks beer.*)

KEVIN: I'd like to be looked after. Hear that, Charles?

CHARLES: I'm taken. And you've got a bearer.

KEVIN: Bearer? I said to him this morning, I said, 'Clean my room up, Cedric, it's a pig-sty.' Know what he said? 'I'm too busy, I'll get my bearer to do it.' The wogs and Chinks all see the day approaching when the British go for good. Don't you, Sidney? (*This is to* LEE *at the bar.*) You'll be sorry then, I'll tell you.

LEN: Ta, Charlie. Just have a lie-down before khana. Don't be long. (*Goes.*)

CHARLES: I'm coming.

(LEN *goes same way as* REG. ERIC *arrives other way, carrying a large tin cylinder which he dumps noisily on the floor.* CHARLES *finishes beer.*)

ERIC: Strewth! Pour me a glass of iced water, Johnny. Had to remain under cover till I saw Reg go to the basha. You know what he's like about anything under the counter.

CHARLES: Erica, what are you up to now?

ERIC: (*Pointing finger*) None of that, Bishop. Nothing queer about me. Anyone says there is gets a bunch of fives.

(ERIC *takes out handkerchief and mops face, neck, arms, legs. His shirt shows great sweaty patches.*)

CHARLES: (*To others*) What have I said?

ERIC: My name's Eric. Or Young. Or Love. Or Young-Love hyphenated. But don't give me any of that Erica stuff, all right?

CHARLES: The lady doth protest too much, methinks.

ERIC: I'm warning you, Bishop.

KEVIN: What's in the tin?

ERIC: Lemonade powder.

KEVIN: Roll on!

ERIC: Wizard scrounge. Made a couple of mates in the other ranks' cookhouse. Bang-on skive. All this cost me was a tin of issue cigarettes.

(LEE *delivers glass of water*.)

KEVIN: You flogging it to the wogs or what?

ERIC: No fear, matey. I'm drinking it. Well, not all of it. You can have some too.

CHARLES: A tinful? That's enough to keep the whole unit in lemonade for a good twelvemonth.

KEVIN: We'll all be home by then.

ERIC: Shouldn't bank on that, chiefey.

KEVIN: What's that mean?

ERIC: (*Opening knife and levering tin lid*) Heard the latest prom?

KEVIN: Don't give me no more of that ropey boat gen.

ERIC: This is pukka. Demob's slowing down.

KEVIN: Ex-air crew and all?

ERIC: 'Fraid so, Squire. Because in case you hadn't heard, the Cold War's hotting up. The Berlin Air Lift and Lord knows what.

KEVIN: I don't mind staying on for another *war*. That's what I joined for, to fight the Jerries.

ERIC: Won't be the Jerries this time.

KEVIN: Makes no odds who it is. Long as I get a crack at someone. Chinks, wogs——

ERIC: Oh, dash it, look at that, broken my penknife now. Cheap Chinese rubbish. Borrow your screwdriver, Kevin?

KEVIN: You touch my stuff you get a boot in your marbles.

ERIC: Steady the buffs. Charles, I know *you've* got a knife.

CHARLES: Wrong again.

ERIC: (*To* STEVE) You, what's-your-name, Steve?

STEVE: Sorry, not a thing.

ERIC: (*Sudden outburst*) Right, I've got your numbers. You've had your ruddy chips. Just come whining to me for lemonade, see what you get. A bunch of fives!

(ERIC *picks up tin, with difficulty, and carries it off to billet*.)

CHARLES: (*Following*) Now don't get in a paddy, Love, you know how it aggravates your prickly heat.

(KEVIN *and* STEVE *watch them go*.)

KEVIN: Old Charles takes care of all of us. Male nurse he was.

STEVE: He looks a bit of a homo.

KEVIN: Oh, he's raving. But faithful to poor old Len.

STEVE: Is Len a homo too? As well as puggled?

KEVIN: He's easy. He's got a wife in Blighty. But he likes to be looked after. Don't we all?

STEVE: Not by a bloke.

KEVIN: You got a bint at home?

STEVE: Girl I write to.

KEVIN: Me too. Mine's at school. All love and kisses and current affairs but I have the odd wank over her photo. Funny thing, I've never had a white bint. You?

STEVE: No.

KEVIN: Plenty of chinks, one or two Malays, the odd wog and a few Anglos. But when it comes to white bints, I tuck in my mosquito net and think about Rita Hayworth.

STEVE: Don't we all!

SCENE FOUR
Les Girls

Musical intro behind this and he sings a verse, Gene Kelly style. During this song, curtains close behind them.

KEVIN: When things are getting kinda tough
And maybe I feel I've had enough,
I shut my ears and close my eyes
And turn on my Technicolor paradise.

STEVE: When the mercury starts to soar
And I can't keep control any more,
I study the cinema magazines
Imagining all those glamour queens.

KEVIN: (*Chorus*) In my mind there's a movie show
Of the kind I can always go

24

To find my favourite Hollywood star
From Lana Turner to Hedy Lamarr.

Night and day on that silver screen
Alice Faye can be heard and seen
STEVE: And Lena Horne's waiting patiently
Till Lauren Bacall's had enough of me.

KEVIN: Some of them are wrapped in sable,
Some can hardly move for pearls;
Paulette Goddard—
STEVE: Betty Grable——
BOTH: All the world's most glamorous girls.

Left alone I would stay for good
In my own private Hollywood
And I'd never let the curtain fall
On this million-dollar carnival,
The movie to end them all!

(*They are now joined by* ERIC *and* CHARLES *and sing:*)
QUARTET: Shady joint, street of sin,
Silken stockings, old Berlin,
Ich liebedich, auf wiedersehen,
Damen und Herren, it's Marlene!

(*Tabs open on art deco outlines, drifting smoke,* TERRI *as
Dietrich in* Blue Angel, *straddling a bentwood chair.*)
TERRI: In a sleazy cabaret
Where the clients were so pally
Once I sang the night away—
That's become the Karl Marx Allee.
Danke schön, comrades, danke schön.

Once I sat across a chair
Drinking schnapps from dirty glasses;
Now it's Friedrich Engels square,
Strictly for the working classes.
Danke schön for nothing, comrades, danke schön.

I can't run in heels like this,
So come on, boys, one last kiss.

Danke schön for nichts, Kameraden, danke schön.
Auf wiedersehen, etc.

(*Men shoulder* TERRI *and carry him upstage. Tableau. Curtains.*)
(STEVE *remains downstage. Speaks to audience.*)

STEVE: Dad will, I am convinced, insist on knowing the whys and wherefores. SADUSEA is a small part of a large transit camp. Each pair of men shares a room with a balcony, from which one can look down on the small marquee which is our dining-room, with its adjacent ping-pong table and piano. You can imagine how your sybaritic offspring enjoys the unwonted joys of his new life: good food, an occasional gin, and above all freedom from parades, guards, inspections and the like. As for the personnel of this *outré* establishment, it has its usual quota of illiterate morons but also quite a few pseudo-intellectuals. One of these is Captain Dennis, who may be a genius but it's too soon to judge. I will write more tomorrow after seeing him tonight in the dress rehearsal of his show at the Garrison Theatre. I wanted to dash down these first and no doubt erroneous impressions. Love to you, Dad and Graham, who looked a lot older in the last snap you sent. I shan't be able to call him Tich any more. Yours, Steve.

(STEVE *goes off as* REG *comes on other side, furtively. He watches* STEVE *go, then turns to audience.*)

REG: They must think I'm a bloody zombie. A moon man. Royal Army Service Corps? A likely story. Special Investigation Branch, if I know anything. Well, Private Flowers, you'll need to get your knees very brown to catch me. And I hope wherever they train you spies they pay attention to your weapon training. You're going to need it.

(REG *turns and goes, unsteadily to Chinese percussion.*)

SCENE FIVE
Beginners, Please

Tabs part on TERRI's *dressing-room. A table to one side with electric bulbs round a mirror.* TERRI *as Dietrich is sitting at table with glass of spirit, lighting a cigarette. Percussion ends. Knock on door.*

TERRI: Come in, if you're pretty.
>(STEVE *enters uncertainly, dressed KD.* TERRI *looks him over.*)
>Quite right. Pretty as a picture.

STEVE: You told me to come round half-time and you'd clear my chitty.

TERRI: Sometimes I go too far.

STEVE: So you could accept me on your strength.

TERRI: D'you think we've time before 'beginners'?

STEVE: Then you said you were going to think how to use me in the show.

TERRI: Well, now, let me see.
>(TERRI *takes off top hat and puts it on table, leaves on wig, during this scene he changes from this into the uniform of a Royal Naval Rating. It is done in a way to frighten or excite Steve. He pours a glass of gin, gives it to* STEVE.)
>Drinkie?

STEVE: Thanks.

TERRIE: You see, we're a bit short on the technical side.

STEVE: I thought Len Bonny did the stage managing?

TERRI: Leonora can't really cope. She's like my mother in the old folks' home, forever losing her teeth or catching fire to her knickers. But. Charlotte insists her hubby comes along when we go on tour and the poor thing's fairly harmless, so life's too short for dramas of that kind. Where she *is* quite useless is as company manager. Someone to arrange things, fix the meals, the sleeping quarters, see we've got a practical piano. Could you cope?

27

STEVE: You mean: could I handle the business end?

TERRI: (*Ogling*) You come right out with it, don't you?

STEVE: I think I could, yes.

TERRI: Then, dear heart, you're engaged.

STEVE: And what should I do in the show?

TERRI: Well, a bit here, a bit there.

STEVE: That's all right. I don't expect to hold down any big parts right away.

TERRI: Few of us are that lucky.

STEVE: That's part of the job, isn't it? My father's always telling me that.

TERRI: She knows her onions, then. You'll play as cast, with or without drag. That means wearing frocks.

STEVE: Mister Dennis, I think it's only fair to warn you I'm not a homosexual.

TERRI: Don't worry, love, it won't show from the front.

STEVE: Obviously there are quite a few homosexuals here, which is perfectly all right as far as I'm concerned——

TERRI: Bona for you——

STEVE: But I'm not at all that way inclined myself.

TERRI: Oh, I can see. You positively shriek butch from every pore. But then you can't always judge a sausage by its foreskin. Half the rough trade walking about you'd never tell was gay.

STEVE: Sorry?

TERRI: Why d'you think they call it the *Royal* Navy? It's all part of life's rich tapestry, ducks, the gay panoply of the passing years.

(TERRI *has removed the stockings, suspenders, etc., and the female face but retains wig. He now stands and takes off the dress, revealing a tanned body naked but for bikini briefs. He moves across, passing close to* STEVE, *who recoils.* TERRI *stares at him.*)

You flatter yourself. No one's that irresistible.

STEVE: I was only getting out of your way.

TERRI: We know what you were doing, Ada. You thought I was after your nuts. (*Hangs dress on rail and takes sailor costume, begins putting it on.*) Stephanie, didn't you say? Pour me another gin, dear, and have one yourself.

(STEVE *goes to table and obeys.* TERRI *watches.*)

I bet the future Mrs Flowers can't wait for the day she
sees you standing there with your discharge in your hand?
Eh? That's better. You've got a *nice* smile, you should use
it more often.

STEVE: There isn't any future Mrs Flowers. Just a pen friend.
A schoolgirl.

TERRI: So you're not keeping yourself? In that case, I suppose
you're down Racecourse Road every night touching up the
Taxi Girls——

STEVE: Quite a few of the bods do but I find that such a squalid
transaction. Putting love on a commercial basis. Have you
read *Mrs Warren's Profession*?

TERRI: That Bernadette Shaw?

(STEVE *takes* TERRI'S *drink to him and returns to table to pour
his own.*)

What a chatterbox! Nags away from asshole to breakfast-
time but never sees what's staring her in the face.

STEVE: Oh, I couldn't agree with that. And if she'd chosen to
place that story in Singapore, she—he—might well have
pointed out that we are a colonial power exploiting subject
races by making their women sell themselves to the
occupying——

TERRI: But she never even lost her maidenhead till she was
fifty-eight or something. Are *you* a virgin, sweetie?

STEVE: Me? No! Not really.

TERRI: You can talk to your auntie, dear. I know what it's like
when you're young. The pressure to be a big strong man. I
went through all that. My father thought the ultimate in
masculinity was to stick your chopper into anything that
wore a skirt.

STEVE: Mine isn't at all like that. In fact, I've never thought of
him having sex at all.

TERRI: I tried not to disappoint my father, much as I disliked
her. God knows I tried! I remember as though it was
yesterday the first time I got my hand on a girl's tit. In a
cinema, it was, in Accrington.

29

(TERRI *has now got on the bell-bottoms and takes off the wig and puts on the sweater.* STEVE *sits at table, facing away, gulping gin and pouring another glass.*)

I got my arm round the other side but I found I couldn't do much with that so I started on the near side with the free hand. The first discovery was that it was all soft.

STEVE: Didn't you know *that*?

TERRI: I was never quite sure till then that tits didn't have bones. Anyway. Next I twiddled with the nipple for a bit.

STEVE: Through her dress?

TERRI: Under her jumper. I'd pulled her bra down on my side.

STEVE: Did you like it? Twiddling her nipple?

TERRI: It was a lot like tuning a wireless.

STEVE: Did *she* like it?

TERRI: God knows. I looked at her face from time to time but she was staring at the screen as though she was hypnotized. I began to wonder if touching their tits sent them into a coma.

STEVE: Not as a general rule, no.

TERRI: Anyway I sat there holding this great thing in my hand, in agony with pins and needles, but it seemed rude to put it back so I kept on squeezing and tweaking till suddenly the lights went up and I dropped it like a hot brick.

STEVE: Didn't she react at all?

TERRI: She looked at me and said, 'That was smashing, I liked the ending, how about getting me a choc-ice?' And while I was queueing up, I thought to myself; Ada, that's strictly not for you.

(*Now dressed as a sailor,* TERRI *has moved towards* STEVE.)

STEVE: Well, it is for me. If only I knew *how*.

TERRI: Don't you then?

STEVE: Well . . . several times at home I got a woman in my upstairs room . . . used to get in a hell of a state with ears all red and hair messed up . . . I could undo their bras all right . . . got my hand up their skirts once or twice but— what d'you do after *that*?

TERRI: Are you asking *me*, duckie?

(STEVE *moves from the chair and* TERRI *sits to finish his face.*)

I gather you're supposed to titivate the clitoris.

STEVE: Yes, but where *is* it?

TERRI: Search me.

STEVE: When sergeant majors say, 'You'd know it if it had hairs round it', the fact is most of us wouldn't.

LEN: (*Off*) Second half beginners, please.

TERRI: (*Calling*) Merci blow-through.

STEVE: Even when I dream there comes a kind of fade-out, like a film. Sometimes I feel I'm going to burst. Let's face it, I'm twenty. In most societies by now I'd have been *married* several years. I better get back to my seat.

(*While they talk,* TERRI *signs* STEVE's *form. With eyebrow pencil.*)

TERRI: Enjoying it?

STEVE: I think it'll go down very well.

TERRI: I get a bit puffed these days. Too many Churchmans, too many choppers. Here. And if I were you, some day soon I'd pick up a Chinese girl in the Happy World. They're professionals, dear, they've even got a union.

STEVE: Yes, but I feel that physical love must grow from personal affection, there must be——

TERRI: Leave your name and number, duckie, we'll be in touch.

(STEVE *smiles, makes for door, staggers slightly.*)

Ooops.

STEVE: Not used to all this gin.

(STEVE *goes.* TERRI *checks appearance in glass, then turns to audience.*)

TERRI: I was like her once upon a time, believe it or not. Romantic, idealistic. Nothing sordid or unforgivable could happen. Nobody could break your heart, nobody could use you or degrade you or steal from you or chuck you off like an old pair of drawers when they'd finished with you. But after one or two had trampled over me on their way up the ladder, I thought to myself, 'Ada, you're becoming a soft touch,' and from that time I played it for pleasure, never fell in love and rarely got hurt. A short life and a gay one. I had a fabulous time, and let's face it I gave good value. Pretty as paint and witty with it. Then just before the war I fell in love again, this time for keeps. And what did he have to be? A matelot, of course. And what was he on as soon as it started? Atlantic convoys, naturally. And how long was it before the U-boats got him? Just over a year. The next-of-kin were informed, his wife and his mother, but I had to hear it a long time after from someone off the same ship in a gay bar.

(*Cloth has come down behind him, lights have gone, but for spot on him.* TERRI *claps his hands.*)

So. Boys and girls. What you're going to see now is my own dance fantasia dedicated to the memory of all the boys in navy blue who laid down their lives for a better, freer, gayer world. And also to the women and children and the poor old queens who waited for them at home. Thank you. (*Lights out.*)

SCENE SIX
Western Approaches

A piano concerto begins, pastiche-Grieg, Rachmaninoff and Gershwin. Cloth goes.

Spot on SYLVIA *in belted raincoat, headscarf and ballet shoes. Lights on backcloth representing a stormy sky.* SYLVIA *mimes and dances, signifying by looks at her watch, etc, that she is keeping a rendezvous. Change in the music brings on* KEVIN *in polo-neck sweater, cap, dark trousers.* SYLVIA *backs away but* KEVIN *pursues, rips off her headscarf and her long hair falls free. Exit barred other side by* CHARLES, *dressed like* KEVIN. *Flashes on skycloth as she runs from the rapists and they throw her about, Apache-style.*

TERRI *leaps on as matelot and saves her. Attackers produce knives but he disarms them and sends them away, one injured.*

The violence gives way to a lush melodic theme as they dance their love in full stage lighting but this is soon interrupted.

REG: (*From audience*) Take your coat off!

(*Dance continues uneasily.* REG *claps hands, standing in an aisle.*)

What's she wearing a raincoat for?

TERRI: (*Coming front*) What's the matter?

(*Music stops.*)

REG: During the rape Miss Morgan's coat ought to be torn off.

TERRI: This isn't a striptease.

REG: Steady on, Terri. I only said the coat. I want to see the dress underneath. This number's gloomy, you need a splash of colour.

TERRI: But Reggie dear, this isn't a colourful number. It's meant to be in muted tones.

REG: The boys up-country want a splash of colour.

SYLVIA: This is symbolic, don't you see that? I'm not only meant to be a girl being raped. On an altogether deeper level I represent a fleet of merchant ships.

TERRI: I shouldn't bother, duckie——

SYLVIA: Charles and Kevin are U-boats and Terri is the Naval convoy that beats off their attack. After which he and I continue our vital journey across the Atlantic. My Lord, I should have thought *anyone* could see that!

REG: Well, perhaps I don't know much about art——

TERRI: (*Spinning round*) Who said that? How dare you!

REG: —but your ordinary squaddie will see this as a rape. And in a rape they'll expect a lot more torn off than a headscarf.

TERRI: Reginald, I hope you aren't trying to teach your auntie to suck eggs because I've been in this business all my life——

REG: And look where you've finished up——

(*For once* TERRI *is silenced. Out of it* SYLVIA *speaks.*)

SYLVIA: You will kindly apologize for that remark.

REG: (*Arriving at steps to stage*) What did you say? I'll what-did-you-say?

TERRI: (*To* REG) You dare shake your handbag at me! An officer and a lady!

REG: (*Climbs unsteadily to stage*) Are you giving me bum-boy lip? Are you?

(REG *staggers towards* TERRI.)

B

SYLVIA: He's been drinking. He can't see straight.

   (CHARLES *and* KEVIN *are onstage now, watching.*)

REG: Can't I? I can see you, black as you are. And remember this, I don't take cheek from the Bombay Welsh.

   (SYLVIA *slaps his face.*)

   (*Raising hand*) By Christ!

STEVE: (*From audience*) Don't you touch her!

REG: Who's that?

STEVE: (*Arriving onstage*) You better not.

REG: As you were, sonny. I've already warned you——

STEVE: And I'm warning you.

   (STEVE *staggers too.*)

TERRI: She's pissed as well.

REG: One step out of line, you'll be RTU'd.

STEVE: You people think you can tell the world what to do.

REG: I'll throw the book at you, make no error.

SYLVIA: Whoever you are, please don't risk trouble.

STEVE: I don't care. They can't be allowed to tell creative people what to do——

REG: All right, soldier, I've cautioned you. Don't imagine being a spy can frighten me. You're Returned to Unit.

CHARLES: He's only just arrived.

TERRI: Sergeant Major, I'll say whether Private Flowers's going to stay or not. Don't forget I'm an honorary captain and if there's any more sauce I'll have you on the carpet, though quite honestly I don't fancy it.

REG: You better lock me up. You better put me under close arrest because if you don't I may do something I'll regret. I may strike an honorary captain and that could mean a court martial.

TERRI: Oh, come on, give us a kiss and make friends——

REG: I mean it! Put me under close arrest.

TERRI: Jessica Christ! Well, how do I do it?

REG: Get two sergeants to escort me to the guard room.

TERRI: Kevin and Charles, arrest the sergeant major and take him to his quarters——

REG: Not them! They can't, they're improperly dressed!

TERRI: Really! (*Calling.*) Len, Eric, come on here!

(ERIC *enters in Scottish costume, kilt, sporran, etc.*
LEN *follows in drag—crinoline, powdered
wig, etc—carrying usual clipboard*)

ERIC: I don't think I can make that change in time——

REG: D'you call that properly dressed?

CHARLES: Steve's the only one who is.

ERIC: What's going on?

REG: He's a private. He's not a substantive sergeant.

TERRI: Have a heart, Reg, where can I find a substantive
sergeant at this time of night?

KEVIN: I'm a substantive flight-sergeant.

LEN: You're dressed as a fucking U-boat.

REG: There's an enormous transit camp out there, with a
sergeants' mess not fifty yards off.

TERRI: Steven, would you be a dear. Run out and fetch me two
properly dressed substantive sergeants——

REG: Warrant officers.

TERRI: Warrant officers then.

STEVE: What shall I tell them?

TERRI: Say we want to arrest our sergeant major but the only
officer's dressed as a sailor and one of the sergeants is in a
crinoline and in any case——

GILES: (*From auditorium*) Thank you, Mister Dennis.

TERRI: (*Peering out*) Who's that?

GILES: Major Flack.

REG: Company, Commanding Officer on Parade, atten-tion!
(*The service personnel obey as best they can.* GILES *wears
major's insignia on KD, carries a walking-stick; a spare
ascetic man, authoritative, quiet, with the air of an earnest
scoutmaster.*)

GILES: (*Coming down aisle on to stage*) Stand easy. I'm afraid
you've had an uninvited audience for this particular
turn——

TERRI: You're always welcome, Major, I've told you——

GILES: Not me. There's been a huddle of transit camp personnel
at every window of the hall.

REG: Sarnt Bonny, detail some men to close the shutters.

GILES: I've already packed them off. But I'm afraid they've seen

35

this sketch or whatever it is you're practising. And most of them found it amusing so I suppose you know what you're doing . . .

TERRI: This isn't a sketch, Major, only a difference of opinion.

SYLVIA: Sergeant Drummond wants to see a rape. He says all the boys want to see me being raped and in a rape my raincoat would be torn off. But this is not a rape, Major, it's a choreographic fantasia.

REG: I only want the coat removed in order to countercheck the wardrobe requisition.

TERRI: Right, come on, sweetie, take it off! Give him the strip-tease then perhaps he'll let us polish off the *pas-de-deux*.
(TERRI *and* SYLVIA *unbutton the coat, showing that she's only wearing briefs. All the men but Giles stare at her, the only woman.* SYLVIA *closes her eyes,* TERRI *covers her with the coat and she leaves the stage, crying.*)
(*To* REG) Satisfied?

REG: No. Where's the dress?

TERRI: I never asked for a frock for this number, lovie, only a mac and headscarf.

REG: Sarnt, you got that requisition?
(LEN *provides the clipboard, which* REG *shows* GILES.)
Here we are, sir. Dress satin scarlet one, comprising skirts full one, bodices low-cut one, Western Approaches Ballet for the use of.

GILES: Is that your signature, Mister Dennis?

TERRI: (*Glancing*) Let's face it, if you're going to take us back over every bleeding form we've ever signed! I'm an artiste, not a haberdasher!

GILES: Surely it must be clear even to an ar*tiste* that equipment supplied out of public money must be accounted for and having been provided must be deployed to maximum advantage. Whether it's a battleship or a ball-gown. Extravagance is always bad thinking. Signifies luxury. And we know what luxury leads to: the Russian Revolution. The fall of France.

TERRI: But Jesus Christ, I didn't ask for the silly frock!
(*Pause.* GILES *draws himself up, glances at the men.*)

GILES: Neither does being an ar*tiste* justify casual blasphemy. Especially from someone who might be expected to set his men an example of respect for his God and king. Whenever anyone swears by our Saviour we take another step towards barbarism. Let none of us forget that we are here on God's work.

(GILES *is now addressing everyone onstage.*)

We defend a righteous flag and we bring the news of Christ's mercy to peoples who have never known it. Otherwise what are we? At best unwelcome guests, at worst unscrupulous invaders. Sarnt Major, dismiss the company and parade again tomorrow morning for further practice.

REG: Sah!

(REG *salutes and* GILES *returns it.*)

Company, attention! By the right, dismiss!

(GILES *goes first with* REG, *then others shuffle off, leaving* TERRI *alone.* LEN *lets in front-cloth behind him while* TERRI *speaks to us.*)

TERRI: And she swept off with Regina and left me feeling about this small. Well, it didn't say anything in my contract about setting an example. There was no work in England, the panto season was over and life under Clementina Attlee wasn't exactly the Roman Empire. So I signed on for sun and fun. With never a mention of God or Georgina the Sixth. And I certainly got what I came for. Singapore, 1948, and they'd booked me in at Raffles. Antiquated even then but terribly Somerset Maugham. Only snag, it was out of bounds to other ranks. Luckily my room had a balcony with an easy climb from the garden. And most naval ratings are very nimble nipping up the rigging after weeks afloat doing the Captain Bligh stint. Then, to a mature woman, how romantic, standing in the moonlight saying, 'Matelot, matelot, wherefore art thou, matelot?' Though not all my rough trade were prepared to climb that far for their oats and then I envied Sylvia her tatty little room where she could entertain to her heart's content.

SCENE SEVEN
Get up them Stairs

Lights come up behind cloth showing it to be a gauze. The scene revealed is a city room with painted backcloth of Singapore's skyline through the window.

Room also has two doorways, one bead-curtained, the other with closed door. Otherwise: double bed, wicker armchair, small record player, over the bed a mosquito net, tucked up.

STEVE *sits on edge of armchair, drinking tea and smoking cigarette. Tray of tea-things is on bed.*

TERRI: (*Continued*) I'd found him comforting her in the dressing-room so pulled my honorary rank and detailed him to escort her home. Which may cause a few of you to shriek 'Get Ada, doing her martyred bit!' But I've never mixed work and pleasure and I had more than I could manage without interfering with minors.

(STEVE *awkwardly hunts an ash-tray and finally drops ash on floor, and rubs it with his foot as* SYLVIA *enters through bead curtain with a plate.*)

See, now she's helped young love to have its fling,
'Tis time your Fairy Queen was on the wing!

(TERRI *entrechats into the wings as the cloth is flown and* SYLVIA *stops in passing to look through the window into the street below. From there we hear the night sounds of Singapore: Malayan song, car horn, etc, then she continues to* STEVE.)

SYLVIA: Hey, listen, I found a few Lincoln Creams. D'you like them?

STEVE: Thanks.

SYLVIA: They're my favourites.

(STEVE *takes and eats, while* SYLVIA *sits demurely on the bed, wearing a modest dress and slippers.*)

More tea?

STEVE: I'm all right, thanks very much.
(*A church clock strikes two quarters of the Westminster chime.*)
Church bells!

SYLVIA: St Andrew's Cathedral.

STEVE: Church bells on the Equator! What a grotesque
anachronism!

SYLVIA: I bet it reminds you of home? Yes?

STEVE: Yes.

SYLVIA: (*Listening*) Now they're gone and we're back to trishaw
bells.

STEVE: Churches go with bike-rides in country lanes . . . and
cold mornings with smoke from bonfires . . . apple
crumble . . .

SYLVIA: Shepherd's pudding.

STEVE: Anything to do with being cold . . . rough heavy clothes
and blankets pressing down on you at night . . . baths as
hot as you can stand . . .

SYLVIA: I know. Like a hill station.

STEVE: Suppose so, yeah.

SYLVIA: Didn't you ever go to the hills where you were in India?
Simla, Naini-Tal, Darjeeling? Oh, you missed something,
let me tell you! But when we're touring up-country we
might visit the Cameron Highlands. They say you have log
fires there and girls need to put on stockings and cardigans.
I'd be like that girl you told me about that's waiting for
you at home.

STEVE: She's only a woman I write to. She's not waiting for me.
She gets a bit lonely and sends the news——

SYLVIA: Lonely? In England? Now, come you're pulling my leg,
if a person's lonely there surely they'd go to their club?
Surely they'd stroll along the Strand to Pall Mall for a
drink in one of the clubs?

STEVE: In London. Yes. But this is in *Swindon*. (*Eats biscuit.*) I
was in a *Youth* Club.

SYLVIA: There you are. That's like the Junior Carlton. And later
on you'll move on to the proper grown-up club in St
James's.

STEVE: I don't know London all that well. I used to stay with
  my auntie in Wood Green. I don't think she was in a club.
SYLVIA: It's nothing to do with where. My father was born in
  South Wales and *he* belonged to a club.
  (STEVE *shakes his head, mystified. He sips tea.* SYLVIA *goes to
  look out of the window again. He shyly turns to watch her.*)
STEVE: Has it stopped?
SYLVIA: What? Oh no, it's still raining cats and dogs.
STEVE: I better go just the same.
SYLVIA: (*Returning*) Hey, listen! Do you know the Mumbles
  Pier?
STEVE: Where's that?
SYLVIA: You've never been to Swansea?
STEVE: No.
SYLVIA: Never been from Argyle Street to Mumbles Pier on the
  Mumbles tram? Along the front past the Patti Pavilion,
  through Oystermouth to the big hotels?
STEVE: (*Shakes head*) Have you?
SYLVIA: That's no joking matter, Steve.
STEVE: I wasn't joking.
SYLVIA: All my life I've wanted to go. Good Lord, Mummy and
  I used to talk by the hour of how we'd go for tea at Lyons
  Corner House before taking in a show at Covent Garden.
STEVE: I've been to the Corner House. They've got a gypsy
  orchestra.
SYLVIA: (*Snappily*) Who doesn't know that!
STEVE: How do *you* know it if you've never been?
SYLVIA: Daddy told me. And what he couldn't tell us, we could
  read in *London Illustrated News*. Look! (*She pulls a large
  black tin trunk from under the bed.*) Mummy's trunk. It
  went with us round all those countless military cantonments
  in India.
STEVE: I've got one of these. Whose address is painted on top?
SYLVIA: My grandma's in Swansea.
STEVE: Why didn't you ever go?
SYLVIA: A chapter of accidents. We were in Bangalore when war
  broke out. The regiment had been posted home and
  everything was packed. Daddy was killed soon after in

Burma. We lost our married quarters and had to manage on a sergeant's pension. Luckily Mummy was a very great snob and had paid for me to take ballet at school so this was the start of my dancing career.

STEVE: (*Reading trunk lid*) Not Wanted On Voyage.

SYLVIA: That only means it goes in the hold of the ship.

STEVE: I know. *I've* got one. We've *all* got one.

SYLVIA: D'you know Mummy's worst day? When we left Calcutta to come down here. 'It's the wrong way,' she kept saying, 'it's further East.'

STEVE: Why didn't you stay there?

SYLVIA: After the British quit? After Partition? What for?

STEVE: We shall be quitting this place too. Not before time either. Then you can all get on with running your own countries. Indians, Chinese, Malayas, Burmese . . .

SYLVIA: I'm not any of those. Not even one of the professional Portuguese Eurasians. What shall I do, d'you think? Move on to Hong Kong?

STEVE: Go to England.

SYLVIA: Eight thousand miles. Have you the slightest idea how much that costs? In any case, all these people aren't *ready* to rule themselves.

STEVE: They'll learn.

SYLVIA: Look at India. Out of the frying-pan into the fire.

STEVE: Education is everything, Sylvia. Once they understand, men will stop worshipping gods that don't exist and learn to love one another and that will mean the end of war.

SYLVIA: Tell the truth, I don't give a damn what happens to all these primitive countries, as long as I get to Swansea and see my grannie before she dies. Poor Mummy never went. Never even saw the Boat Race except in Gaumont British News.

(SYLVIA *has moved to the window again and stares out.*)

STEVE: What is it you keep looking for? Out the window?

SYLVIA: I thought I heard a car. Did you hear it?

STEVE: I can hear lots of cars. (*He moves to join her, looks out.*) Thought you said it was still raining. I better get off.

SYLVIA: Where's the fire, for heaven's sake? I know what you'd like. Some jazz.

(SYLVIA *goes to gramophone and looks at records.*)

STEVE: No, honestly——

SYLVIA: Or would you rather have Ralph Vaughan Williams?

STEVE: Got to catch the liberty gharry back to camp. Don't want
to get stuck in town all night with nowhere to kip. Get
picked up by the redcaps.

(SYLVIA *goes to record player and starts a record.* STEVE *puts
on his beret and tidies himself.*)

SYLVIA: One for the road? A gin and it? A nightcap?

STEVE: Thanks for the tea and biscuits.

(*Music: Paper Doll.* STEVE *makes for door.*)

SYLVIA: Thank you for seeing me home. And for coming to the
rescue of a lady in distress. I hope you don't get into hot
water.

(*She kisses his lips.* STEVE *hesitates then goes and* SYLVIA *closes
door behind him. She makes at once for the window, looks out.*
STEVE *comes on from side of stage, watching her.*)

STEVE: . . . quite honestly, Heather, I'm afraid you'd think a lot
of the people here lah-di-dah and a lot of the things they
say unnecessary. But there are so many different sorts of
people about with different ways of looking at things . . . it
is going to be an enormous task educating them all, even if
the teaching profession is bursting with brilliant geniuses
like yours truly.

(SYLVIA *waves from the window then collects the tray and goes
out by the bead-curtain doorway, as front-cloth comes down on
the room.*)

If only you could be here for a day so I could show you
how little there is in common between Singapore and
Fernleaze Crescent. But do keep writing with the news. We
all long for the mail to come and you can imagine that the
unfortunate wretch who receives no letter is a prey to
morbid imaginings and nervous breakdowns. Love and all
that, your itinerant but ever-faithful, Steve.

(*Music. Curtains part.* STEVE *goes.*)

SCENE EIGHT
Forces Sweethearts

TERRI *appears wearing long white dress and wig, seated writing letter.*
On the desk a lighted candle. On the refrain the men hum to his singing.

TERRI: My dearest, I'm writing once again
From the still of my lonely room
And dreaming of the moment when
We'll stand as bride and groom.
For though today you're oh-so-far-away,
I imagine all we'll do and say.

When the shadows creep
Over fields of sheep
With a love that's deep
You and I will go to sleep
Doing all those little things we used to do.

When the chapel bell
Says 'good night, sleep well'
To the wishing-well
And the children's carousel,
We'll do all those little things we used to do.

Remember September,
The country weekends,
The yearning we felt inside?
And autumn recalls
Such wonderful balls,
The organ at eventide.

We'll be true until
In a church that's still
I shall know the thrill
Of whispering 'I will',

Then we'll do those little things that we
used to do before
But with roses around the door.

(*Accompaniment and male chanting goes on through next
speech.*)
Darling, do you remember VE Night and VJ Night, how
we danced and sang in the streets? The bonfires and the
crowds? Everyone felt so glad peace was here again and we
could all get on with the job of building anew? But in
three short years the world is once more torn by strife and
that's why boys like you have got to be over there keeping
the peace till everyone's come to their senses again. And
then, dearest, there'll be so many wonderful things to do
together and a whole lifetime to do them in.

Remember December,
Those Christmases past,
The mistletoe where we kissed?
The carols, the tree,
Your presents to me,
The stuffing we couldn't resist?

(*They all sing the final stanza.*)
ALL: On a day new born
In a field of corn
There's an April morn
When we'll welcome in the dawn
Doing all those little things that we used to do before
But we'll do them forever more.

(TERRI *goes and music ends. Lights now reveal a row of
cubicles upstage.*)
(STEVE, KEVIN, CHARLES *and* ERIC *are preparing to take
showers. They have been singing with* TERRI *on the last refrain.
They are wearing only towels round their waists.* LEN *enters,
also in towel, with mail for them. Others have drinks.*)
LEN: Letter for you, Charlie, from Yorkshire. Fucker for me and
all from the fucking wife.

44

CHARLES: Gawd help us. My Mother. The voice of doom.
  (LEN *gives out letters as he names them.*)
LEN: There, Wimbledon, cop hold of that. One from your young tart.
ERIC: Bang on, Squire.
LEN: Einstein, fucker for you. Lambeth, there's even a cunt for you.
KEVIN: I wish there was. A nice white one.
  (*All look at their mail, settle to read and give extracts aloud.*)
ERIC: This is from Susan all right. Wizard!
KEVIN: My young lady pen-friend. 'Dear Kevin, thank you for the snap you sent. How brown you look! Am I right in saying you are something like Gene Kelly only younger?'
LEN: 'My dear hubby, not much to write about as per usual. Aldershot is much the same and most things rationed still even bread now, it makes you wish old Winnie was back and all parcels very welcome as per usual . . .'
STEVE: Bloke in my basha in Bukit Timah, got the boat before I was posted here. 'Remember I promised I'd write and tell you what it's like when you get home? Well, the worst is there's no boat to look forward to. When you're in, getting out becomes a kind of religion but what can you do when paradise turns out to be a dead loss?'
ERIC: 'You will see from the background of the enclosed snap that New Malden is as beautiful as ever.' (*Looks at snap.*) Not only the background, but Susan in the front. (*Kisses photo, goes on with letter.*) 'The cherry blossom makes you wonder what they mean by a Cold War but Dad says it's all due to the miners not being able to dig enough coal to warm it up, however much they get paid. He keeps us in fits with his jokes.'
LEN: 'Do you remember Corporal Pratt that we knew in Iceland?' I remember him, the randy cunt. 'He has turned up here, what a small world . . .'
KEVIN: 'When you go swimming do watch out for those man-eating sharks you wrote about in your last . . .' (*Stops, looking nervously at others but they aren't attending.*)
STEVE: 'My family are entirely concerned with trivial domestic

45

problems. I am having to accept the fact that I've grown up
and they haven't.'

ERIC: 'Mum says she can't make out why our boys in the RAF
are dropping food on Berlin when it seems only yesterday
they were dropping bombs . . .'

LEN: 'Working in the NAAFI is very hard on nylons and I see
where you are getting an increment in your overseas
allowance. Do let me have a pound or two to buy some
clothing coupons on the black market and oblige your
loving wife Valerie . . .'

CHARLES: So she can oblige Corporal Pratt, I imagine.

LEN: You wouldn't fucking knob it. What's your mother got to
say?

CHARLES: Auntie May's had a prolapse, Dad's having a stone
removed, her feet are playing up. It's more like the *Lancet*
than a letter.

LEN: (*Calling*) Couple of tigers, chop-chop, Johnny.

ERIC: 'But my brother Doug says if we care anything about
democracy we've got to give one in the eye to Old Joe
Stalin. He's doing ever so well now, by the way, with that
big American oil company.'

CHARLES: Her brother Doug, does she mean?

KEVIN: 'We are doing Malaya in Geography and I asked Miss
why you're out there and said it was to do with letting
Stalin have some rubber.' (*Looks up.*) That's not right, is it?

STEVE: 'And you needn't think you are going to impress people
with your uniforms. They couldn't care less. They don't
even know there *is* an army in Malaya.'

ERIC: 'Your friend Corporal Lawrence hasn't come here yet to
deliver the silk for my wedding dress. Princess Elizabeth's
marriage set me looking forward to ours all over again . . .'

KEVIN: Not even sent a photo this time.

(CHARLES, LEN *and* STEVE *finish their letters silently and go
into the shower cubicles upstage. Sounds of water continue
behind dialogue.*)

ERIC: Susan has.

KEVIN: (*Taking snap*) That her?

ERIC: That's my bit of kaifa, matey, waiting for me in New

Malden.

KEVIN: You'll be all right there. Bit like Deborah Kerr, is she?

ERIC: All right? Is that all? I'll be laughing, mate. In the lifeboat. Asbestos.

(KEVIN *returns snap, goes into cubicle.* ERIC *reads on.*)

KEVIN: You going to know what to do, though? You don't want to disappoint her first time. You come down Racecourse Road one night, let some Chinky tart show you what to do.

ERIC: No fear. I'm staying clean for Susan.

KEVIN: Bit of practice do no harm. And as for them stories, that's all bull. Chinese twats go the same way as white ones.

LEN: How d'you know? You ain't never had a fucking white bint.

KEVIN: I seen them though. I got sisters. Here's a better idea! How d'you fancy a touch of Black Velvet? Old Sylvia now? She's a good sort. Clever too. They reckon she can smoke a cheroot in her minge.

LEN: Blow smoke rings and all, can't she?

KEVIN: Used to do it in Calcutta, didn't she, for the Yanks? In a cabaret?

(STEVE *comes out and begins towelling.*)

LEN: Takes some fucking muscle control, mind.

CHARLES: You're pathetic, both of you, with your tatty fantasies.

KEVIN: You want to teach your Susan that.

ERIC: (*Threatening*) Now watch it, Lambeth.

KEVIN: Go down well in New Malden.

ERIC: I've warned you——

KEVIN: The Young Conservatives' Garden Party.

ERIC: (*Out of shower*) Talk as dirty as you like about half-caste tarts but start on Susan and see what you get——

KEVIN: (*Coming out*) What then? What? Come on! What?

ERIC: (*Showing fist*) A bunch of fives! That's what.

CHARLES: Not again! If Love came to visit you in *hospital*, he'd bring you a bunch of fives.

ERIC: (*Turning on him*) I'll deal with you in a minute, Bishop.

(KEVIN *has grabbed his towel and flicks it at* ERIC'*s buttocks.*) Right, that's it. I've ruddy well warned you, Cartwright, now you're for it——

(ERIC *grabs his own towel but* KEVIN *pulls it from him and*

throws it into the cubicles, continues to flick at ERIC *with his own.* KEVIN *gets photo of Susan and mimes masturbation.*)
You've had your chips, chiefy, mark my words—hey, steady on, that hurt——

(*The others are all out by now and have towelled and put on their towels.*)

(REG *enters, properly dressed, with cap.*)

REG: Company, attention! Officer Commanding!

(GILES *enters, as men come to attention.* KEVIN *quickly wraps on his towel.* ERIC *is left without and has to find his in the cubicles. Then he tries to wring it out while* GILES *waits in silence.*)

Hurry it up, there.

ERIC: Sah!

(ERIC *finds and wraps towel around him, comes to attention.*)

GILES: Carry on, Sarnt Major.

REG: Last night's guard detail, one pace forward—march!

(ERIC *smartly steps forward, stamps with bare feet and his towel falls off.*)

Pick it up, man, pick it up! (*And as he does.*) Name and number.

ERIC: 2231747, Acting-sergeant Young-Love, sah!

GILES: You were on guard duty last night?

ERIC: Sah!

GILES: And do you remember my staff car leaving my quarters some time after midnight?

ERIC: About two hundred hours, sir, yessir. I saw you coming, lifted the barrier and presented arms. You acknowledged the salute, sir, in the back seat.

GILES: No.

ERIC: Thought you did, sah.

GILES: I wasn't in the back seat. I wasn't in the car at all.

ERIC: Your driver certainly did, sir.

GILES: That wasn't my driver, that was a Chinese communist.

ERIC: Sah?

GILES: He was stealing my car, Sarnt. We cannot say for what reason. It was later found burnt out on the Bukit Timah Road.

48

(Silence. CHENG comes on bringing glasses on tray. He moves about and REG notices him.)

ERIC: I recognized your car, sir, I naturally thought——

REG: Can I offer you a drink, sir?

GILES: A lemonade, thank you.

REG: Cheng, two lemonade chop-chop. Use that tin of powder you've got behind the bar. Savvy?

(CHENG goes with tray.)

GILES: Now I understand the guard for our compound is drawn from transit personnel. So why were you, an acting NCO, patrolling our lines?

ERIC: Volunteer, sah. I've volunteered for permanent Friday night guard duty.

GILES: What for?

ERIC: *(Shrugs, attempts pleasantry)* Keeps me out of trouble, sah.

GILES: Not on this occasion.

ERIC: I mean it stops me spending money in the mess, sir, or Singapore. I'm saving all my pay towards my marriage.

GILES: I wish you every happiness.

ERIC: Keep myself very busy, sir, all through my service. Volunteer for everything: firefighter, assistant in the early treatment room, clerk to the Catholic padre, dog-shooter, magician, anti-malarial officer——

GILES: Magician?

ERIC: In the show, sir.

GILES: Ah.

CHARLES: He makes cars disappear.

(Men laugh. GILES stiffens.)

GILES: You wouldn't find it quite so funny if the communists had burnt your billet with you inside. Or lined you and your family up against a wall and sprayed you with machine-gun fire. That's already happening, d'you know that? Not only to British planters but Indian managers, Chinese business-men, Malayan farmers. Anyone's fair game! As you were. Anyone who doesn't want Asia becoming part of Stalin's back garden. Anyone prepared to save Malaya from a new dark age of atheism. That is what we're here for. And that is why we'll stay.

49

(CHENG *has returned with two glasses of lemonade.*)
Thanks, boy. Stand at ease, men. Stand easy—Now—
though I myself am a life-abstainer, I never object to
moderate drinking in others. So finish your beers by joining
me in a toast.
(*The men get their glasses,* REG *and* GILES *the lemonade.*
CHENG *stands waiting.*)
To the defeat of communism in South East Asia Command
Malaya and Singapore and the victory of Christian
enlightenment!

MEN: (*Mumbling*) To the defeat of communism in South East
Asia Command Malaya and Singapore and the victory of
Christian enlightenment.
(*They all drink.*)

GILES: Excellent lemonade. Now some of you may be saying,
'Yes, that's all very well, but law luv a duck, we're only
peace-time conscripts waiting for the boat back to dear old
Blighty.' And others may say, 'Just a tick, sir, this is a
non-combatant unit after all.' But, as we see from last
night's episode, we *are* a military target. And if we don't
defend ourselves, no one else will. From now on we're not
relying on transit personnel to patrol our perimeter. Mister
Drummond's drawn up a roster for the coming months.

ERIC: Sir! I'd like to volunteer for permanent Saturday night
guard duty as well——

REG: Not a chance, Love, you've had your chips.

GILES: We must encourage keenness, Sarnt Major. And I don't
think Sarnt Love can be singled out for blame. Any of you
might have done as he did. We've got slack, that's all.
Singing and dancing's all very well but it won't stop
communist Chinamen.
(CHENG *has moved about collecting glasses.* GILES *finishes his*
drink, returns glass to him.)
That's all, men.

REG: Company, attention!
(*The men come to attention.* ERIC's *towel falls off.* GILES *makes*
to exit but pauses, sniffing the air.)

GILES: Do I smell women's perfume?

REG: There's a distinct suggestion of it, sir.

GILES: I hope you're none of you allowing women in these quarters. Strictly out of bounds.

REG: I don't think it's women, sir.

CHARLES: It's mine. I wear it.

GILES: Bless my soul! What for?

CHARLES: My part in the show, sir. Female impersonation.

STEVE: We all do, sir.

GILES: You're the new man, aren't you?

STEVE: Sarnt Flowers, sir.

GILES: Settling in?

STEVE: Yes, thanks very much.

GILES: All right. No perfume on guard duty, eh? No mufti either. Properly dressed, fixed bayonets. But—— (*to* CHARLES) well done, Sergeant. That's the kind of keenness we like to see, isn't it, Mister Drummond?

(GILES *goes and* REG *comes straight to audience. Cloth down behind him.*)

REG: Talk about the three monkeys! He's the lot rolled into one. Bum-boys crawling out the woodwork and he doesn't even see. Still. I got rather more pressing problems. Such as what to do about our pet spy from the Special Investigation Branch. He plays it very sweet, I must say. Butter wouldn't melt in his back passage. But not quite crafty enough. They'll have to get up very early to catch me. Dead or alive. (*Goes, threateningly.*)

SCENE NINE
Harmony Time

Cloth flown, blackout. In the dark Kevin's face appears, lit by a single torchlight from beneath. He sings to the tune of 'Greensleeves'.

KEVIN: There was a dusky Indian maid,
      In old Bombay she plied her trade

51

And in Calcutta and Bangalore
And in Government House she was called Lahore.

(*Other torches now light the faces of* TERRI, CHARLES, LEN,
ERIC. *They form a male voice choir.*)

CHOIR: Black Velvet was full of joy
For every British soldier boy.
She guaranteed to please
And the most that it cost you was five rupees.

There came a soldier-boy fully grown
Who till that moment had held his own.
And though he'd served on several fronts
He'd never seen action on ladies once.

Black Velvet had great allure
For such a private, so young and pure.
She took him well in hand
And showed him the way to the Promised Land.

She took off all her seven veils
And then she told him she came from Wales
And how she'd seen the Forth Bridge one day
While gazing out across Tiger Bay.

Meanwhile she softly read
The Khama Sutra from A to Z
And after that was done
They started again at Chapter One.

(*Lights have come up on* SYLVIA's *room. The tin trunk is
standing by the bed. The mosquito net is down, draped along
the upstage edge of the bed.* SYLVIA *and* STEVE *are lying naked,
partly covered by it and a sheet. She is downstage of him,
lying face down, sobbing.*)

STEVE: What is there to cry about? Sylvia! I thought you liked
it. I thought you said——

SYLVIA: Of course I liked it, good heavens above! But that
doesn't ever make it *right*. What sort of a world would it
be if everyone just did as they liked?

STEVE: I thought that's what it's all about. I thought that's why we're out here. Defending freedom.

(SYLVIA *sniffs and wipes away her tears with a corner of the sheet.*)

SYLVIA: How can you ever respect me again?

STEVE: I don't respect you. I love you.

SYLVIA: I'd rather you didn't send me up.

STEVE: I'm not sending you up. I *love* you. I must have told you a dozen times in the last hour how much I love you.

SYLVIA: But every man says that when he's doing jig-jig.

STEVE: Does he?

(*Pause.*)

SYLVIA: Well, doesn't he?

STEVE: I don't know. It was my first time.

SYLVIA: Oh, good grief! I thought you were inexperienced but oh, that makes me even more ashamed! You must have thought me a real woman of the streets!

STEVE: I knew it wasn't *your* first time——

SYLVIA: Try to understand that a woman on her own——

STEVE: —but that was all to the good. You made it seem so easy.

SYLVIA: I didn't lead you on, you must admit that——

STEVE: All those years being frightened to death! All those years I could have been doing it, wasted! If you and I had met in Calcutta, we could have started then! We could have been at it for two years!

(STEVE *kisses her shoulders, neck, and back.* SYLVIA *turns over to face him. He goes on kissing her body.*)

SYLVIA: Oh, Steven, have a heart. You can't make up for twenty years in one night.

STEVE: These bruises. Do they still hurt?

SYLVIA: No, not at all. I'd rather you didn't pass remarks about them.

STEVE: Was it during a performance you fell?

SYLVIA: A rehearsal. It's nothing. I told you——

(SYLVIA *gets up suddenly, wraps a kimono round her and goes to the window. She leans out, looking and listening. We hear the trishaws, cars, etc.*)

STEVE: Listening at the window again? What for?

SYLVIA: I came to close the shutters, would you mind? It's

hotter of course but you can't hear those Chinese sounds so much. You can imagine you're anywhere but Singapore. (*Closes shutters.*) I play English records and pretend I'm living in Regent Street.

STEVE: Do you really want to go to England? Or is that only pretend?

SYLVIA: I'm afraid you're a very heartless boy under all that lovey-dovey talk. Do I want to go! Not Pygmalion likely. (SYLVIA *shakes her head and goes to the gramophone, looking through a pile of records.* STEVE *sits up.*)

STEVE: But I mean *really*. I mean, if you were the wife of a British soldier, they'd have to take you, wouldn't they? (SYLVIA *pauses, then continues looking at the records.*) D'you want to go enough to marry me? There wouldn't be all that danger to you. Because if you didn't like me afterwards, we could be divorced. Of course I'd try to keep you because I meant what I said, while we were doing jig-jig. I loved you before and I love you even more now.

SYLVIA: Not like you? Why shouldn't I like you?

STEVE: (*Shrugs*) You've lived so much! The daily round of a teacher's wife wouldn't be all that glamorous!

SYLVIA: Glamorous! Would you mind kindly telling me what's glamorous about a dancer's life? Every dirty old man putting his hand up her skirt? Trying to get her to do disgusting things for American soldiers.
(*Pause.*)

STEVE: What kind of disgusting things?

SYLVIA: Hells bells, I don't know. *I* didn't do them.

STEVE: I never said you did. But what *kind* of things?

SYLVIA: Suggestive things.

STEVE: Some of the bods were talking, they said a woman can smoke a cigar—you know, not in her mouth——

SYLVIA: Are you trying to change the subject?

STEVE: What? No. I want so much to marry you, Sylvia. Of course before you committed yourself, we'd have to make sure the army would, in fact, pay your passage. I'll ask Sarnt Major Drummond.

SYLVIA: No!

STEVE: He's i/c Admin.

SYLVIA: No, Major Flack. Your commanding officer must grant you an interview on personal grounds. That's in King's Regulations.

STEVE: All right. I'll say, 'Permission to marry Miss Morgan, sah!' And if he says what for, I shall say, 'So that I can go to bed with her every night, sah! And every morning and every afternoon, sah!'

SYLVIA: Just you dare!

(STEVE *is caressing her again, beneath the kimono. He leads her towards the bed but she breaks away.*)

I'm going to put a record on. You'll enjoy doing it to music.

STEVE: First of all I must use the gents.

SYLVIA: A little pee-pee and then more jig-jig.

(STEVE *goes by curtained doorway.*)

I'll put on something to remind you of England.

(SYLVIA *winds gramophone and puts on orchestral version of 'Greensleeves'. Calls to him as she moves away.*)

You've missed the liberty gharry. You'd better stay the night now.

(SYLVIA *performs a few dance movements as the door opens and* REG *comes in, dressed in uniform KD. He sees at once that she's alone. She freezes.*)

You shouldn't just walk in like this. I feel I've got no privacy.

REG: That's American. Privacy. You better say privacy if you want to pass muster in the Burlington Arcade.

SYLVIA: Please, Reg.

REG: Wherever did you learn that? Privacy!

(REG *moves across and as he passes* SYLVIA, *she flinches. He pauses then continues to the gramophone, takes off the record roughly.*)

SYLVIA: Please go.

REG: I got no choice. My flat's being watched. They've got spies on me at camp. They're closing the net. Get me a drink.

(REG *crosses to the wicker chair, sees the KD uniform on it, looks up at her.*)

SYLVIA: I've got company.

(STEVE *comes in by curtained doorway. Pause.*)

STEVE: Hullo, Chiefey.
REG: I *see.*
(*Blackout.*)
(*Torchlight on faces as before. They sing again.*)
CHOIR: She demonstrated the Clinging Vine
    And quickly taught him the Sixty-nine.
    She showed him some of the ways there are
    That a lady can draw on a man's cigar.

    Exhausted she turned away
    Saying, 'I've not had a lie-down all day,
    Have pity on my poor feet,'
    But the soldier-boy outflanked her line of retreat.

    In came the sergeant and nearly burst
    When he saw the private had got there first.
    He said, 'I'll have you on close arrest,
    You're out-of-bounds and improperly dressed.'

    Then warmly the soldier swore,
    'My dear Black Velvet, I love her sore.'
    'Sore, are you?' the sergeant said,
    'Then you've picked up a dose in that old bag's bed.'

    Black Velvet shouted, 'Do stop it, boys,
    Indeed to goodness, let's have no noise.
    Instead of making a brouhaha
    Why don't we arrange a ménage-à-trois?'

    Now see our soldiers twain
    Serve with all their might and main,
    One occupying Madras
    And the other one holding the Khyber Pass.
(*Torches out.*)

SCENE TEN
Our Sergeant Major

REG *enters without shoes.*

REG: (*Turning from choir to us*) I don't think!
(*Front-cloth comes in but unlit. Only spot on* REG.)
Well, it had to happen, you knew that. Once they set their
spies, they wouldn't take long. But fancy those two being
so close. I confess that possibility had never crossed my
mind. He's as fly as they make them, that one, pretending
he'd been slipping her a length. Excuse my French but
I'm under pressure. (*Suddenly shouts.*) Lee!
(*No response.*)
I suppose they think they've got me by the short and
curlies. But I'm an ex-copper. They'll find they'll have to
get their knees brown before they take me. (*Moves, thinks
again.*) As you were, her knees *are* brown! She's brown all
over. Except for where she's black-and-blue. That was an
error, I see that now. I lost control, but I was provoked.
She pushed her luck too far . . . I won't have pushy tarts
on my patch. Still, it was a mistake. D'you think that was
the day she shopped me to the SIB? (*Suddenly shouts.*)
Cheng!
(*No response.*)
All right. So they've searched my flat, I can't go to Sylvia's
room, they've even taken my revolver from the billet. I bet
they think they've got me over a barrel. Maybe they have
but just you watch it, Private Flowers. Don't go up any dark
alleys.
(LEE *appears, white shirt and shorts, bringing boots, puts them
on* REG'*s feet.*)
Where you been? When Boss call you come chop-chop,
savvy? Or else you come intellogation room bimeby

morning, plenty why-how-where.

(LEE *nods*.)

You tell bearer he leave plenty shit on shoes. You tellum Sahib see him mollow morning after him see dhobi-wallah. But my wear boots now, him velly big hully. You find Cheng, bling my room. My got plenty trouble. Need help. Catchee monkey. Savvy?

(REG *goes*. LEE *remains*.)

(*Lights off front-cloth and we discern through gauze some vague jungly outlines, hanging strips denoting trees, foliage, etc.*)

(*Chinese percussion during* REG's *exit gives way soon to sound FX: mostly heavy rain but also dog bark, night bird, etc.*)

(*Long flash of lightning reveals a figure in bush-hat and monsoon cape crossing stage. In the darkness the* SOLDIER *stops under hanging tree. From under cape he brings torch and by its light he leans rifle with fixed bayonet against the tree. Then he looks at his wristwatch, then switches off.*)

STEVE: 'Dear Heather, in your last missive you remarked how much you envied me the lovely tropical sunshine. As I seem to remember you being top of our class in geography, perhaps——'

(*A whistle nearby silences him. He looks towards the place, then moves a few steps, shines his torch.*)

Hullo? Anyone there? Um—who goes there?

(*Flash of lightning shows him facing one way while behind him* CHENG *comes in and takes his rifle and goes.* STEVE *waits, then returns to position.*)

'. . . perhaps you will recall that Singapore's climate is characterized by far heavier rainfall than you ever get in Fernleaze Crescent . . . tonight, for example——'

(*A cry, human or animal, from the jungle, like a laugh.* STEVE *pauses.*)

'. . . I am on guard duty in a virtual deluge which means standing under a tree with a rifle and fixed bayonet for two hours at a——'

(*Movement on the far side of stage and a flashlight beam.* STEVE *shines his beam towards it. He and* ERIC *are revealed in each other's beam,* ERIC *in hat and cape, with gun.*)

ERIC: Hullo, Swindon?

STEVE: Love! What you doing creeping about like that?

ERIC: I wasn't creeping. You should have challenged me. I could
have been the Sarnt Major.

STEVE: You don't think Reg would ever come out in this!

ERIC: I've got news for you, my old oppo. He's just been round
the guard room. Had a cup of char with us then said he
was going to take a shufti. You haven't seen him?

STEVE: No.

ERIC: Dead lucky I was. If he'd come a few minutes sooner he'd
have caught me standing in the rain, bollock-naked.

STEVE: What for?

ERIC: Trying to cure my prickly heat.

STEVE: I'd sooner have prickly heat than pneumonia.

ERIC: Mine's not just any old prickly heat, matey. It's the worst
case in the whole of South East Asia. The MO told me
I've actually got prickly heat on my prickly heat.

STEVE: The only way is stop sweating.

ERIC: My dear old mucker, I can't help sweating.

STEVE: Yes, you can. Relax. Stop panicking. Stop trying to be
what you're not.

ERIC: What's that?

STEVE: One of the boys.

ERIC: A sure sign of a good education is that one's able to muck
in with all sorts and conditions of men.

STEVE: It makes you look a nana.

ERIC: Watch it, Swindon! I've got your number, matey.

STEVE: And I've got yours! But for you making such a cock-up,
we'd none of us be standing out here in the pissing rain.

ERIC: Well, you can go for some kip right now. I'm not stopping
you. I'm *relieving* you.

STEVE: None too bloody soon either.

(*A sudden shout offstage from* REG.)

REG: Halt! Who goes there?

ERIC: (*To* STEVE) It's Sarnt Major Drummond.

STEVE: Is he talking to us?

REG: Halt! Who goes there? Friend or foe?

ERIC: Friend! It's us, Chief—Young-Love and Flowers——
  (*A shot and a cry from* REG.)
STEVE: Christ! Where's my gun?
  (STEVE *goes to look for it while* ERIC *blows a police whistle very loud.*)
  It's gone. My rifle's gone!
ERIC: What?
STEVE: Give me yours.
ERIC: No fear.
STEVE: We've got to go and look. And you can't see to shoot with all that water on your glasses.
  (STEVE *tries to grab gun but* ERIC *struggles, then loses.*)
ERIC: All right, I've got your number, you're for the high jump——
STEVE: Shine the torch, for Christ's sake . . .
  (*They advance thus upstage into the trees,* ERIC *shining torch,* STEVE *holding rifle at the ready.*)
  Reg . . . you all right?
ERIC: Sarnt Major . . . shout if you hear us . . .

SCENE ELEVEN
Lest We Forget

Chinese percussion. Rain stops.
Bright lights on front of cloth.
LEN *marches on, KD, carrying clipboard. Comes smartly to the halt, faces front and looks at board, frowns, mouths the words, looks up again, turns to give orders to the wings.*

LEN: Come along, there, let's be having you, get fell in!
  (KEVIN *and* CHARLES *enter, KD, casually, counting money.*)
KEVIN: What's up, Len?
LEN: You're supposed to be on parade.
KEVIN: What for?
LEN: So I can pick the guard of honour. The fucking cortège.

60

So stop fucking about and form up.

CHARLES: Two of us can't very well form up. Couldn't we just gather round?

LEN: The others'll be coming, soon as they've been paid. Major Flack has detailed me as senior NCO——

KEVIN: You're not senior NCO, I'm senior NCO.

LEN: D'you want the fucking job? You can have the fucker.

(KEVIN *shrugs, goes on counting money, puts it away. Enter* ERIC *and* STEVE, *also counting money.*)

Get fell in, now, I'm looking for four volunteers to carry the bier. (*And as they make boozy noises.*) The fucking coffin!

ERIC: (*One pace forward*) Sarnt!

LEN: You sure you wouldn't drop it, Wimbledon?

CHARLES: You've no choice, Len, everyone else is out on tour. Put me down too.

LEN: (*Writing*) Ta. (*Reading.*) It would be highly advantageous if the bearers were of roughly similar height.

(KEVIN *bends knees.*)

Can't you show some fucking respect for your dead fucking comrade?

KEVIN: What's this pantomime got to do with respect? The best respect we could show old Reg is revenge, mate. Revenge on the slant-eyed sods who killed him. You ask for volunteers for that, you can put my name at the top.

CHARLES: That won't bring him back.

KEVIN: Like it says in the Bible though, an eye for an eye, a tooth for a tooth. Give them what they gave him. First a bullet, then cut their heads off. Who's with me?

ERIC: I'm with you, Chief.

STEVE: And me.

LEN: And all of us I dare say. But first we got to bury our dead. Parade tomorrow nine-hundred hours. And just remember this will be tantamount to a church parade. So best behaviour, mind. No acting like cunts in the house of the Lord.

(*Drum beat begins. They turn and march off. Lights change. Cloth flown. Bare stage.* LEE *and* CHENG *come on upstage, drab clothes, with shovels, and prepare a grave trap.*

Meanwhile TERRI *comes on front in officer's KD with black arm-bands.*)

TERRI: We were all ordered on that parade. I thought of wearing the little black number from our Latin-American medley but no, it had to be the full captain's drag with only a discreet arm-band. I chose the fairly butch day-slap, no rouge or lipstick and the merest suspicion of eye-shadow. Well, funerals and weddings play havoc with mascara.

(*The drum starts again, now muffled.* LEN *leads on the cortège. Slow-marching with a rifle. The coffin is draped with the Union Jack.*)

And as soon as the Tiller Girls carried her in, there wasn't a dry eye in the cemetery.

(GILES *follows KD, with sword at present. Bearers turn upstage and place the coffin over the trap.* SYLVIA *is last, also in black. All arrive at trap as the bearers lower the coffin on ropes.*)

When the padre said, 'In the midst of life we are in death', I thought well, many a true word spoken in jest. And as they lowered the coffin, I'll swear every one of us was trying not to imagine that decapitated corpse inside.

GILES: In sure and certain hope of the resurrection to eternal life, through our Lord Jesus Christ . . .

(LEN *fires a round into the air.* TERRI *puts hands on ears.*)

TERRI: They always do that, apparently, when some queen's given her all on active service. I said, well I've done that many a time and never got more than a port-and-lemon.

(TERRI *goes upstage to join the funeral group. Mourners throw earth on coffin. Muffled drum resumes and the bearers slow-march away.* LEN *brings flag and men bring poles. Chinese shovel earth into the trap.* GILES *comes down to address audience as lights go and cloth comes down.*)

GILES: Stand at ease, men. We mourn the loss of our comrade-in-arms. Both as a man and a non-commissioned officer, Mr Drummond deserved the admiration of us all. Not least in his attention to detail. Nothing was too trivial, be it the display of a dress on the stage, the insubordination of a native bearer or the prevention of rabies. He was not, by his own admission, a God-fearing man. Indeed, fear was not in his nature. But in his care for you young men, his concern that none of you be corrupted by waste or idleness, he retained many qualities from his previous service as a London bobby: dependability, discipline, devotion to duty. This devotion it was that led to his savage murder, for it was he who posted the guard after my car had been stolen. And he who went out in heavy rain to inspect that guard and came instead upon the gang of communistic Chinamen who shot him. I need hardly remind Sergeants Flowers and Young-Love that after killing him they hacked his head off. They will never forget the sight of that mutilation.

(GILES *pauses, clears his throat, moves and resumes.*)

It should not have needed this atrocity to awaken us to our danger but it has. Like the British here in Forty One, Forty Two, drowsily playing cricket on a lawn beside a Gothic Cathedral. And if you'd said, 'But look here, you should be arming yourselves, the yellow men are on the way,' they'd have answered, 'My dear chap, Britannia rules the waves, remember. If their tinpot ships try to sail into Singapore, our great guns will pick them off like pigeons.' Well, as you know, our friends from Tokyo came the other way. Down through the mainland riding bikes. Across the causeway, ting-a-ling, 'Velly solly, no more clicket now.' It's not funny, Sergeant! Let us give thanks to God for this ghastly warning. Heaven be praised we've heard the bicycle bells in time. And look here, it makes no odds that this is a song-and-dance unit. Never send to know for whom the bells toll. They toll for *thee*. Me. All of us.

GILES *opens hymnal and sings. Men join in second verse.*)

GILES : Behold! the army of the Prince of Peace,
       Conquering that His kingdom may increase,
       Taking to some distant Asian shore
       His cleansing and redemption evermore.

ALL : Many a laughing savage lives and dies
       In ignorance of Jesus' sacrifice

And sun-kissed children swing beneath the palms
Hid from the mercy, mercy, mercy of His loving arms.
Amen.
(*They go.*)

SCENE TWELVE
Tea for Three

Cloth up on SYLVIA'*s room. Percussion continues. She's sitting on bed,
still in black. In the wicker armchair is* CHENG, *white shirt and
trousers. There is a tray of tea-things on the tin trunk and they are
both drinking from cups.*
STEVE *opens door and enters, wearing* KD. *Sees* CHENG. *Music stops.*

SYLVIA: Hullo, darling.
(STEVE *leaves door open, comes forward, takes off beret, staring
at* CHENG.)
The Major kept you a long time. What did he have to say?
(*No answer.* STEVE *stares at* CHENG, *who stands, finishes tea.*)
Are you going, Mr Lim?
(CHENG *puts cup on tray, bows to her, then him, goes to door but
she follows.*)
You won't need to come again.
(CHENG *shakes his head, smiles, goes.* SYLVIA *shuts door.* STEVE
throws beret down, moves up to window, looks out. SYLVIA
moves towards him.)
Terri dropped me here right after the funeral. I thought
you'd be coming straight away. I kept on my dress so that
you could take it off.
(STEVE *continues round the room, away from* SYLVIA. *She
follows some way, then goes to pour tea.*)
I'm also wearing the black underwear we bought in the
shop in Stamford Road, d'you remember? You came into
the cubicle to give me your opinion and—well, frankly, it
was so enthusiastic, so—noisy, goodness only knows what

the assistants thought. I could hardly look at them after-
wards . . . my face was so red.
(SYLVIA *now approaches* STEVE *with cup of tea.*)
Darling——
(STEVE *takes tea, sips it, looks at it, makes sour face.*)

STEVE: What's this? Where's the milk and sugar?

SYLVIA: You don't have milk or sugar with China tea.

STEVE: China?

SYLVIA: Lapsang Suchong. Fortnum's sell it in Middle Road.

STEVE: You sit here with a bloody Chinaman drinking China
tea, still wearing the dress you wore to Reg's funeral!
Why didn't you get the bloody *China*man to take it off?
(STEVE *throws cup and saucer down.*)

SYLVIA: Steve, you're not jealous?

STEVE: Jealous? God Almighty, what's jealousy got to do with
it? I'm talking about being British. All right? Because,
whatever you say, you're not—not by a long chalk. Not
that I give a damn, and when everybody's been educated,
of course, there won't be any patriotism and colonies and one
race fighting another . . . but that's a long way off and
whether I want to be or not, *I'm* British. I realised it when I
saw Reg lying headless in a pool of rain. And Major Flack's
been talking to us and he made me see we're on one side
and the Chinks are on the other. And then I find you
actually being touched up by that slant-eyed fuck-pig.
(STEVE *takes up the tray and throws it across the floor with a
clatter of tin and broken crockery. For some moments he
stands.*)

SYLVIA: Mr Lim came here to see Reg. He didn't know of his
death but was very happy when I told him.

STEVE: I'll bet he was! They're happy to hear any British
soldier's dead.

SYLVIA: *I'm* glad they killed him too. Many people will be
celebrating tonight.

STEVE: I'm not saying he was a saint. I didn't even like him. He
was a bully and a drunk and he had a down on queers and
Indians but I never heard he cut off anyone's head.

SYLVIA: You're like Mummy. She thought he was the cat's

whiskers. 'Play your cards right,' she used to say, 'you could be Mrs Drummond.'

STEVE: Didn't she know he was married already?

SYLVIA: I didn't either. Not till after Mummy's death.

STEVE: But you still went on seeing him?

(SYLVIA *picks up a few bits of crockery.*)

SYLVIA: I told him not to come again as I was not prepared to play second fiddle. He said that wouldn't be possible, he needed this place to meet his clients and associates and I'd be required to entertain them.

STEVE: You mean clients like Mister——?

SYLVIA: Mr Lim was a middle man. A contact with the garment trade, I think. Getting the costumes made for SADUSEA that hardly ever appear on the stage. They were paid for and signed for by the army but most of them were used in Reg's sideline . . .

STEVE: Sideline?

SYLVIA: Boy prostitutes.

(SYLVIA *is sitting on the bed now.* STEVE *goes to pick up pieces of crockery.*)

STEVE: Well, if Reg hadn't done it, someone else would.

SYLVIA: Absolutely.

STEVE: That bloody Chinaman, I suppose——

SYLVIA: Mr Lim didn't enjoy his work.

STEVE: Why did he do it then?

SYLVIA: Reg had some kind of hold over him. Gambling debts, I don't know.

STEVE: What hold did he have over you?

SYLVIA: You've seen these bruises. That was for answering back at the dress-rehearsal.

(*Pause.*)

STEVE: Did he have any other sidelines?

SYLVIA: Import-export. Thai silk, jade and works of art looted from Buddhist temples. It was brought here and sold to private collections in America.

STEVE: Its unique geographical position makes Singapore an ideal entrepôt port. I learnt that in geography.

SYLVIA: Then Reg came along and soon their business expanded into opium and Chinese refugees and gun-running.

STEVE: Gun-running? Come on——

SYLVIA: Only to protect his own interests at first, but then he realized there was a very steady demand from the communists. So he formed another——

STEVE: You're taking the piss. D'you think I'm a moon man? Think I've just come out?

SYLVIA: It's true! Cross my heart and hope to die.

STEVE: If it's not, you'll have a few more bruises to show the next zombie that walks in here——

(STEVE *has left the tray and is now holding* SYLVIA *threateningly by the wrist.*)

SYLVIA: You're hurting my——

(SYLVIA *struggles and bites* STEVE's *hand. He lets go. She moves away. He sucks his hand.*)

He formed another partnership with a captain in the ordnance corps! They supply the communists from the armoury in the transit camp.

STEVE: (*Moving after her*) Proof! You better give me proof or Christ, I'll——

SYLVIA: What? What? Take me to the interrogation room? Why d'you think that had to be whitewashed so often? Because of the bloodstained walls!

STEVE: That only shows he was a bully. Give me proof he was selling guns to the Commies.

SYLVIA: Proof? How can I prove it? D'you think he let me have it in writing? He was an expert at covering his tracks, getting authorization, using the law. He learnt that as a London bobbie.

STEVE: You can't prove it, can you?

SYLVIA: I've just said I can't. D'you think he told *me* anything? I had to piece it together from what I overhead.

STEVE: Like your picture of England. Half-baked bullshit.

SYLVIA: Please don't use language when you speak to me.

STEVE: All made up from bits and pieces. The Mumbles Tram! Lyons Corner House!

(*Pause.*)

SYLVIA: I used to be sent out whenever they got down to

business but I do remember one night, I was out there, Reg was very angry with a Chinese man in here. He was shouting something about the CO's staff car. They must have used it to make deliveries of arms out of the camp and over the Johore causeway on to the mainland . . . then one night on the way back the driver had gone into a tree or something——

STEVE: And the car had been burnt out on the Bukit Timah Road.

SYLVIA: You knew all the time.

(STEVE *slumps into the wicker chair*.)

STEVE: It was after that Major Flack made him draw up a guard roster.

SYLVIA: That's right. He said to this Chinese man it was no thanks to him but the whole incident had turned out well because smuggling the guns would be much easier now you lot were forming the guard.

STEVE: And then one night he's inspecting the guard—perhaps to see if the coast is clear—and——

(STEVE *makes sounds of throat-slitting*.)

SYLVIA: It's an ill wind that blows nobody any good . . .

STEVE: D'you reckon they were genuine robbers or was it an ambush or what?

SYLVIA: He had so many enemies. He was always frightened. His palms perspired dreadfully, did you notice? He thought you were after him, I'm sure. The night he found you here, he thought you were a spy set to catch him. He twisted my arm till I said you were.

STEVE: Why me?

SYLVIA: He used to carry cyanide in case he ever needed a quick way out.

STEVE: He found an even quicker one in the end.

(STEVE *comes to* SYLVIA *and embraces her*.)

Sorry for what I said.

SYLVIA: So you think I'm wrong about the Mumbles Tram?

STEVE: I'm sure you're right.

SYLVIA: *You* were right about Singapore being an entrepôt port.

(STEVE *kisses* SYLVIA, *looks at dress*.)

STEVE: Is this one of those costumes? Take it off.

(STEVE *turns her back and he opens the dress.*)

And don't ever wear it again. Or anything else he gave you.

(SYLVIA *steps out of dress.*)

SYLVIA: All right. Now come to bed . . .

(SYLVIA *goes upstage as lights fade on room, puts on record of 'Greensleeves', pulls mosquito net down and gets into bed.* STEVE *speaks to audience.*)

STEVE: Dear Everyone at Fifty-Six, I'm sorry to hear from Dad that the spirit of post-war idealism hasn't lasted. I still believe education is the only hope for the world, though of course in the light of experience it won't be nearly as easy as I once imagined. In fact, life seems more complicated every day. If one genius may paraphrase another, there are more things in heaven and earth than are dreamt of in Fernleaze Crescent . . . Tell Heather I'll be writing as soon as I——

SYLVIA: Steve! Come on!

STEVE: Must dash now. In haste. Love to everyone. Steve.

(*Goes up to the bed as the music swells.*)

ACT TWO

SCENE ONE
Noël, Noël

TERRI *comes before tabs wearing DJ, carrying cigarette holder and sings the following:*

TERRI: Dear Whomever It May Concern at the BBC,
      Pass this letter to the Brains Trust very urgently.
        Throughout the war we soldiered on
        When almost every hope had gone
        And pinned our flagging faith to Vera Lynn.
        We turned out railings into tanks
        And smiled politely at the Yanks
        When all they sent across was Errol Flynn.
      But when the lights went on we saw the vict'ry was a
          sham,
      The Lion's share turned out to be a smaller slice of Spam.
        The bluebirds came one dreary day,
        Looked at Dover and flew away
        And grim spectators murmured, 'Why can't I?'
        They might go down to the sea in ships
        But that's forbidden by Stafford Cripps
      And the nightingale in Berkeley Square can only sit and cry.

      So—could you please inform us who it was that won the
          war?
      The outcome isn't certain, Heaven knows.
      Now everyone's so keen to put the Germans on their feet,
      For apparently
      The majority
      Are really rather sweet.

Meanwhile back in Britain we're still lining up in rows
To buy enough to keep ourselves alive.
So could you please inform us how we came to lose the war
That we won in nineteen-forty-five?

Land of Clement Attlee
Where the teeth are free!
Our former wealth is going to
Augment the Inland Revenue
And though our situation might seem hard
At least you needn't work these days,
The Ministry of Labour pays
You well, provided someone's stamped your card.

The National Health is failing fast and no one gives a fig,
The Corpses will look delightful in a newly-issued wig.
Our image for posterity
Is one of grim austerity,
The Socialist Nirvana's on the way:
New ministries proliferate
Whose function is to allocate
To everyone his fair and proper share of sweet FA.

Room Five Hundred and Four
Has met a somewhat grisly fate;
Now everything's in duplicate
That fourteenth heaven on the old tenth floor
Is Room One Thousand and Eight.

So—could you please inform us how we came to lose the
        peace?
Perhaps it's best to be the losing side,
Now that the Americans are sponsoring the Japs,
Taking the view
That but for a few
They're awfully decent chaps.
Such a strange development is wounding to our pride,
The countrymen of Wellington and Clive,
So Bevin only knows how Britain came to lose the peace
When she won in nineteen-forty-five,

Four, three, two, one,
Yes *won* in nineteen-forty-five?
(TERRI *goes. Tabs rise or part.*)

SCENE TWO
Kernel of the Knuts

Tabs go up on a backcloth of office/wall, featuring large map of Malaya and photo of George the Sixth. Plain desk and two chairs. CHENG *is onstage pouring tea into cup.* GILES *comes from side, addresses audience.*

GILES: Why did we lose the peace? I can answer that question. There was never a peace to lose. There was only a temporary truce and a slight change of enemy. No sooner had the Yanks exploded that contraption than bands of agitators turned from killing Japs to killing us. Burma, Siam, Indo-China, anywhere they didn't get what they wanted within five minutes, it was 'go home, British'.
(CHENG *brings him tea.*)
Well, now at last it's official—'an emergency' they're calling it but everyone knows it's the start of The Third World War. Soon as——
(LEE *comes on with* STEVE, *who salutes.*)
STEVE: Sergeant Flowers, sir.
GILES: Ah, yes. Stand at ease. I'd offer you tea but it's China.
STEVE: I like China tea, sir.
GILES: Another cup, Ming.
(CHENG *goes.* LEE *stays with third shadowy* SERVANT.)
Sit down.
(STEVE *does but* GILES *moves about.*)
I understand the tour of Singapore Island is being well received.
STEVE: They seem to like it, yessir.
GILES: No accounting for taste. But then I'm no judge. Last

time I saw a show was—what?—1935. Puerile drivel.
Once saw half a film and walked out. Can't conceive why
anyone wastes their time with it when they might be
reading Bunyan or the Bard.

(CHENG *returns with cup and pours for both.*)

Or learning to tell one constellation from another. One
bird from another. Most of them don't know a wren from a
tit.

STEVE: Sir.

(GILES *sits, looks at papers on desk.*)

GILES: Glowing reports on you as company manager. Miss
Morgan, for instance, says you grow more capable every
day. Captain Dennis particularly praises the way you've
handled the business end. Even Sergeant Bonny, as far as I
can make out from his semi-literate scrawl, confirms your
qualities of leadership. Thank you, Ming.

(CHENG *moves up to join others.* GILES *sips tea.*)

Now. As you know there's a war on.

STEVE: You mean the state of emergency?

GILES: That's softly-softly officialese. The communists used to
call themselves the Malayan People's Anti-Japanese Army;
now it's the Anti-British Army. What's that if not a
declaration of war? I immediately applied for posting to an
active command. I pointed out that I'd spent three years in
India and elsewhere preparing to invade Malaya. I'm
trained for this kind of war. I want to serve my God,
my king and my country. Are you a Christian?

STEVE: I was in the choir for a time, sir.

GILES: Churchgoing family.

STEVE: My father manages the local co-op. He believes more in
fair shares, moderation.

GILES: What do you believe in?

STEVE: Well, Education, first, sir, then——

GILES: Not good enough. Why don't you sign on with Christ?
Oh, I know what you're going to say, you're going to say,
'Yes, but look here, I didn't ask him to go and die for me
on the cross like that.'

STEVE: Well, sir, I didn't. I wasn't even born.

GILES: Be your age, Sergeant, look beyond your nose. You'd better start believing in something. We'd *all* better. Because *they* do. The Russians, the Chinese, the Malayan People's Anti-British Army. What, d'you think?

STEVE: Sir?

GILES: *What* do they believe in?

STEVE: Equality, sir? Fair shares? Social justice?

GILES: Precisely. Pie in the sky. Jam tomorrow. Take equality. Think of Sergeant Bonny. Look at Bonny's handwriting. Visualize Bonny's brain. Out of the sewers of Birmingham into the jungles of Malaya. Backbone of the army, of course, loyal to a fault, obedient, dependable. But is Stalin going to give him command of a division out of a belief in equality? Is he? Yes or no?

STEVE: Well, sir, what Marx actually said was from each according——

GILES: No's the answer. Because Uncle Joe is a wily old bounder and Bonny's as dim as a nun's night-light. He might just let him command a latrine. And indeed so would I. No more. So much for equality, a notion by which millions of child-like people are led into prison-camps. Millions of Bonnys. And make no mistake, they must be led one way or another. Either into Siberia or the Kingdom of Heaven.

STEVE: I think, sir, that if education begins early enough——

GILES: You can't educate what isn't there. The Bonnys of this world must be *told*. They *want* to be. Form fours. Present arms. Stand easy. And someone has to tell them. Me, of course. Or Mr Drummond. Or since his death, perhaps you.

STEVE: Me, sir?

GILES: Our unit's strength is short of one sergeant major. I can apply for a new NCO or I can make you up to that rank. How d'you feel about sharing the burden of command?

STEVE: Sorry, sir. Are you——

GILES: I'm offering you a crown. D'you want time to think it over?

STEVE: No, sir. I'd like to help you—like to share the burden, sir——

GILES: (*Shaking hands*) Well done, well done! I shan't pretend this isn't going to be a tough assignment. We may well get into a spot of bother up-country.

STEVE: You mean because of HQ saying we've got to charge admission?

GILES: What?

STEVE: The shows have always been free before, sir, the men may not take to it kindly. I know it's only a few cents but——

GILES: I said *trouble*, son. Bandits, CT's . . .

STEVE: Isn't our tour mostly the coastal area? (*He points to map, west coast of mainland.*) Kuala Lumpur, Ipoh, Penang, Butterworth. Not many bandits there, sir.

GILES: All right. But what do these chaps want with entertainment? Yet another diversion, when they already enjoy the amenities of these large cities? While over here the front-line troops have to go without? (*Shows inner areas to the east.*) Now perhaps it was someone's idea of a joke to give me command of a concert party but command it I do and our itinerary is my business and no one else's. I know more about jungle-fighting than all the desk-wallahs at GHQ. This is the route we'll be following.

(GILES *has unlocked a desk drawer and now shows* STEVE *some papers.* CHENG *comes and collects cups on to tray.*)

Until the Cameron Highlands it's the one Mr Drummond drew up for us.

STEVE: Mr Drummond?

GILES: Yes. But after the Camerons we get off the beaten track. And that's where we may run into trouble. May even go out of our way to look for trouble. We shan't only be playing to British but also Malays and Gurkhas and Indians——

STEVE: Will they understand the show, d'you think?

GILES: Give them a splash of colour, plenty of movement. You've got a conjurer, haven't you?

(CHENG's *gone off with tea.* GILES *locks paper in drawer.*)

STEVE: Yessir.

GILES: Dancing girls?

STEVE: One, sir. Miss Morgan. Matter of fact, that's why I applied for this personal interview. To ask your permission to marry her.

GILES: The Anglo girl?

STEVE: Yes.

GILES: Handsome.

STEVE: I think so, sir.

GILES: Women of mixed blood often are. Early on. Snag is, they
tend to put on weight rather soon. How old is she?

STEVE: Twenty-eight.

GILES: (*Whistles amazement*) That almost certainly means thirty.
When you're thirty she'll be forty. Middle aged. And, of
course, they find it difficult settling down in the UK.
Climate's not what they're used to. They don't like the food.

STEVE: Oh, she's very British, sir. Her Dad was in the Welsh
Fusiliers.

GILES: Welsh and Indian? Combustible mixture. Don't say
anything to her till you're perfectly sure in your own mind.

STEVE: I've already asked her, sir. And been accepted.

GILES: (*Sighs*) She's after a free trip home, you see. Quite a
consideration. On the other hand, they don't take an
engagement as seriously as English girls. Remember you're
going to have your work cut out up-country. You'll need
mens sana in corpore sano. If you understand me?

STEVE: (*After a pause*) A sound mind in a healthy body.

GILES: Yes but do you catch my drift?

STEVE: I'm not sure, sir.

GILES: Difficult. I have no son. Daughters, yes, but my wife
handled all that, of course. How's your French?

STEVE: All right up to School Certificate.

GILES: Alors . . . vous savez . . . physiquement les femmes
orientales sont très belles, très mignonnes, n'est-ce pas?

STEVE: Bien sûr, mon commandant.

GILES: Mais il y a toujours la possibilité d'attraper les maladies . . .

STEVE: Maladies?

GILES: Look, all I mean to say is: mull it over while we're out
on tour. See a bit less of her for a few weeks. Meanwhile
I'll get the wheels in motion for your crown. Wong!
(LEE *comes forward and opens door for* STEVE.)
I needn't tell you this is all top secret. Strictly between the

76

two of us.

STEVE: Sir! And thank you.

GILES: Thank you, Sergeant. Command can be lonely.

(STEVE *salutes*, GILES *returns it.* STEVE *goes.* LEE *remains, hands* GILES *his cap and he comes downstage.*)

Dear Margaret, there's a young soldier here I'd like to invite down to the mill-house when I get home. Decent, intelligent boy, very much the kind I'd have liked as a son, had God so willed. He's in a spot of bother at the moment but I mean to help him out of that. As I would my own. (*Moving off, putting on cap.*) How splendid your roses winning first prize again this year . . .

(CHENG *returns by door. He and* LEE *look up at the other* SERVANT, *who has remained indistinct throughout. He now comes down.*)

REG: (*To* LEE) Okay. Stay at door.

(LEE *goes out.* CHENG *remains.* REG *takes out keys and opens drawer, removes paper. Keeps one copy, puts others back. Locks drawer. Comes to us with paper as lights fade on set.*)

All right, Sergeant Major Flowers. You can piss on the old man, he's a babe-in-arms, but not on me! You know I'm still alive, don't you? Course you do. Anyone trained in intelligence would have seen through the circumstantial nature of Reggie's vanishing trick . . . the missing head, the CSM's flash on the wrist, the widow's identification. Then knowing of the disappearance of a British soldier that same night at Nee Soon, he'd have put two and two together. As you certainly have. (*Cloth falls behind him. Looks at itinerary.*) But this is good news. Enable me to plan the perfect get-together. You and me and our bonnie black Madrassi. (*Stows paper in tunic, makes to go, pauses, and points at audience.*)

And not a word from any of you. Anyone I hear saying, 'Look out, he's behind you', will answer to me. Savvy? (*He goes.*)

SCENE THREE
A Tricycle Made for Three

Cloth flown, furniture removed by CHENG *in black. On to clear stage with night lighting.* LEE *drives a trishaw in which* TERRI *and* SYLVIA *are sitting. Pulls up centre and waits. They get out. Piano plays ballad accompaniment to this scene.*

SYLVIA: Terri!

TERRI: Good night, lovie.

SYLVIA: Thank you. Thank you so much!

(SYLVIA *kisses and hugs* TERRI.)

TERRI: My dear, what have I done? Given you a lift home in a trishaw? You mustn't sell your favours so cheap.

SYLVIA: Oh good heavens, it isn't that! I'm thanking you for bringing Steve and me together and for making me so happy.

TERRI: Oh, there again I was only being the good fairy. I rather fancied her first of all but baby-snatching's not my line and she had so much to learn . . .

SYLVIA: Oh, didn't he? Even now I keep on finding how little he knows. When I told him I was going to have his baby, for instance, he asked me how I could tell. D'you know, he thought babies come out of the woman's stomach? Out of her navel!

TERRI: Feminine hygiene's still no part of an English education.

SYLVIA: Imagine at twenty years of age not knowing that.

TERRI: But anyway she understands now?

SYLVIA: I think so, yes. I did some drawings.

TERRI: And everything's all right?

SYLVIA: He's going to see the Major soon. And, listen, d'you think it's a good idea, I suggested Steve should ask him to be Best Man?

TERRI: Major Flack? Why not indeed?

78

SYLVIA: And how would you feel about giving the bride away?
I've no living relatives here.

TERRI: If I must, but I shan't enjoy it.

SYLVIA: Whyever not?

TERRI: I've only just found you, a partner in a million. And next
we know you'll be standing there with a swollen belly
saying 'I will' to a hushed congregation.

SYLVIA: Will you do it or no?

TERRI: I certainly won't let anyone else.

SYLVIA: Thank you again. For everything.

(SYLVIA *kisses* TERRI.)

TERRI: Good night, duckie.

(SYLVIA *goes.*)

Now what shall I wear? The white suit from the Jolson
Medley would be discreet. Or perhaps a frock? Tremen-
dously dignified, the dark dress with the half-veil, with
everyone whispering, 'Who *is* she?' and, 'It's Greer
Garson!'

(LEE *waiting with trishaw rings bell.* TERRI *turns to him.*)

Thank you, Ada.

(TERRI *climbs aboard.*)

Your Fairy Queen's done all the good she may
So Fleet Club, sweetie, by the shortest way!

(LEE *rings bell and drives off,* TERRI *waving and blowing kisses
to audience.*)

SCENE FOUR
Privates on Parade

STEVE *marches on with S-M insignia, leading squad all in KD:* LEN,
KEVIN, CHARLES *and* ERIC. *Drumbeat as they march.*

STEVE: Squad, eff turn! Eff, right, eff, right. Squad, halt!

(GILES *enters, returns* STEVE's *salute.*)

GILES: Stand the men at ease, Sarnt Major.

STEVE: Squad, stand at—ease!

GILES: The tour of Singapore is now over and the time has come for us to go up-country. Bring a bit of a song-and-dance to those chaps who suddenly find themselves chasing bandits in the ulu. Ulu. That's the jungle. But one or two of you might be saying: 'Yes, that's all very well but half a mo, here's the old man telling us to go up-country, likely to get in a spot of bother with the bandits, while he's here in a cushy billet. Seems the rum kind of a go.' And you'd be right. But I'm not staying here. I'm coming with you. The other concert-parties are in Ceylon and Hong Kong so where else should I be? I dare say one or two of you are thinking, 'Just a tick, what use is he gonna be in a show? Reckon by the looks of him he's got a tin ear and two left feet.' And that again would be good thinking. You must be able to look after yourselves if there's any trouble. And that's where I can help. During the next few days I'll be putting you through a refresher course in basic training: small arms drill, grenade throwing, unarmed combat plus as much of a notion of conditions in the ulu as I can give you before the off. So carry on, Sarnt Major.

STEVE: Sir. Squad, attention! Basic training and jungle warfare, by the right begin!

(GILES *salutes and everyone sings a rousing march, with martial choreography.*)

ALL: Come, see the Privates on Parade,
    You'll say: how proudly they're displayed.
And when we hear the music of a milit'ry band
You'll be amazed how smartly we can take our stand.

    For when the bugles sound attack
    Up goes the good old Union Jack.
You may as well surrender when you hear our battle-cry.
There'll be no more escaping when we raise our weapons high
    And in the Vict'ry Cavalcade
    You'll see the Privates on Parade.

(*Much countermarching to music and they exit leaving* GILES *who detains* LEN.)

80

GILES: Sarnt Bonny, a word with you. As you know, you're in line for another stripe. I've been watching you on the square. Well done. But leadership also calls for qualities of tact, diplomacy, understanding.

LEN: I ain't never gone after promotion——

GILES: So let's suppose we're faced with a tricky situation here and now, shall we? See how we'd cope. Here's a platoon of squaddies lined up and you've got to announce some tragic news to just one man. Here he is in Singapore and home in England his mother has suddenly, unexpectedly died. How d'you break it to him?

LEN: (*After a pause*) What's his name, sir?

GILES: (*Impatiently*) Not important. Charlie Farnes-Barnes. Come on, Bonny, thinking on your feet, another of the qualities of leadership.

LEN: Private Farnes-Barnes, one step forward march. Right, son, pay attention, your mother's dead.

GILES: Hell's bells, man, you'll have him in sick bay suffering from shock. Think of something more subtle, a roundabout approach. Indirect.

LEN: (*After thinking*) Right, squad, pay attention. All those men going to see their mothers next time they're on leave, one pace forward march—as you were, as you were. Where *you* going, Farnes-Barnes?

(*Stares at* GILES *hopefully but* GILES *moves away. Others return, including* TERRI *and* SYLVIA, *carrying rifles.*)

ALL: We are the C of E Brigade,
    We're marching on a new crusade.

(*No lyrics to next couplet but dialogue over marching.*)

TERRI: (*To* STEVE) Vada the little tiaras, duckie.

STEVE: What?

TERRI: The crowns on your sleeve.

STEVE: Oh.

TERRI: Bona. Suits you.

ALL: You'll need a piece of four-by-two
    To get a really good pull-through.
    The enemy's resisting and the trumpet sounds advance
    They'd best lay down their arms because they haven't got

D

a chance
Faced with the cocksure cannonade
Of the Privates on Parade.

(STEVE *puts them through paces as Sergeant Major. Then they exit but* GILES *retains* KEVIN *this time.*)

GILES: More to your liking, Cartwright?

KEVIN: What, sir?

GILES: More like being a soldier?

KEVIN: Oh. Do with a bit more jungle training, not so much bull.

GILES: All in good time.

KEVIN: We don't hold with bull in the RAF.

GILES: You were air crew, weren't you?

KEVIN: Navigator bomb-aimer. I joined under-age to get a crack at Jerry. Soon as I passed out flight sergeant, ready to go on ops, old Adolf packs it in. Right, I thought to myself, see if we can't chalk up a few Nips. No sooner reach Ceylon than Tojo says *he* don't want to play no more.

GILES: My story too. All ready to invade Malaya, then two big bangs and all over. Velly solly, no fight now, all lellow men back to land of lising sun. And as for you, Major, we're giving you a new command, a unique operation covering the whole of South East Asia. Covering it with what, sir? Song and dance, Major.

KEVIN: (*Shakes head sympathetically*) I put in for my release. I said, 'You want a navigator bomb-aimer to drive a lorry for three years?' Jesus Christ Almighty, a few weeks sooner I could have bombed Dresden.

GILES: A word to the wise, Flight Sergeant—

(*Sings:*)

Wise soldiers generally refrain
From taking Jesus' name in vain.
One day you'll need to call him in the clamour of a war
Then he would say, 'Look here. You'd often called on me before.
I'm an extremely busy bloke.
You shouldn't use my name in joke.'

(*Others come on, while music continues.* GILES *watches as they practise unarmed combat, assault course, swinging across on ropes, etc. At end* GILES *orders:*)

Right, well done, fall out, gather round.

(*They obey, crouching downstage facing up, while the Malayan map cloth comes down and* GILES *briefs, using the map and his stick.*)

The Malayan peninsula is slightly smaller than England and Wales and four-fifths impenetrable jungle. Rich in game but also crawling with every kind of hazard—soldier ants, centipedes, scorpions, typhus tics, leeches—and if *they* don't worry you the plants tear your clothes and the grass cuts like a saw. By day it's deathly quiet but at nightfall pandemonium breaks out as all these chaps get weaving on their various chores. Yet the odds are all you'll see will be a few fireflies or the eyes of a panther. Which might or might not be the signals of a Chinese terrorist.

LEN: There's Stone-Age men as well, ain't there, sir?

GILES: A hundred thousand aboriginals have lived here since the dawn of time. Before the Malays, Chinese, Indians or British even heard of the place. The true natives. And whose side are they on?

KEVIN: The commies' side.

GILES: You'd think so, yes. You'd think they'd be on the side of their liberators, their fellow-Asians against the Western imperialists. But no, they're with *us*! And why? Because the Chinamen have taken their jungle from them. Turned them out of their ancient homes. Bad thinking that. Rather have one of those Johnnies beside me in the jungle than half the brigade of guards. Marvellous trackers, deadly with a blow-pipe. If you manage to chum up with any of them, give them some name of your own. In Borneo, my two head-hunters used to answer to Oxo and Bisto, the Bisto kids.

TERRI: But, Major, I'm sure my contract stipulates we'll be doing the Number One Tour and keeping to the main roads. There's nothing about the jungle.

GILES: No need for alarm, Mr Dennis. We'll be following the route taken by the previous parties, the route planned by Mr Drummond. More or less. But: this country is a powder

83

keg, even the main roads are a death trap. Once we're on
the mainland, we'll be in the front line. A theatre of war.
(*They turn and sing to audience, crouching at first.*)
ALL: And when we're standing on parade
Each with his rifle and grenade,
You'll hear the sergeant cry:
STEVE: Presenting arms to the right!
SYLVIA: And all the girls declare they've never seen such a sight.
ALL: To know that God is on our side
Makes every private swell with pride.
We'll press upon our enemy until he's in a funk
And show him it's no easy thing
Resisting British spunk.
He'll feel the forceful fusillade
Of the Privates on Parade.
(*They march off.*)
(*Cloth is flown and lights go down.*)

SCENE FIVE
The Midnight Choo-Choo

*Sounds of steam train heard and clouds of vapour blown about in
flashing lights. Music represents labouring engine and whistle suggests
departing train. All but REG, CHENG and LEE enter in a row, working
arms together like pistons. Gradually they accelerate, singing whistle
sounds together and working way across the stage.*

*They haul a truck representing a railway compartment: bench each
side, table between, windows and corridor upstage.*

*LEE and CHENG come on with large cards naming places on the journey:
Johore Bahru and Kluang. REG follows, dressed like them, with card
naming Segamat. Others continue with Tampin, Kotan, etc. Perhaps
the Malayan map has dropped in behind and their journey is traced by
a moving spot.*

*LEN, KEVIN, CHARLES and ERIC occupy the benches, smoking, playing
cards, etc. CHENG appears in corridor wearing railway cap.*

LEN: Kiswasti you come, Johnny? You want dekko railway
    warrants? You go ekdum sergeant major sahib juldi juldi.
    Doosrah compartment. Burra sahib keep warrants
    sub-cheese fucking sahibs and mem-sahib. You get pukka
    shufti, malam? Tikh-hai.
    (CHENG *nods, goes. Noise of travelling train continues.*)
CHARLES: He was Malayan.
LEN: I know that.
CHARLES: They don't speak Hindustani.
KEVIN: *That* what it was?
LEN: Fucking understood anyroad.
KEVIN: You can't even speak the King's English.
LEN: I can speak the king's fucking English better than any
    Cockney fucker, now then!
KEVIN: Not without effing and blinding every other word.
CHARLES: Right. Time for another five minutes with the swear-
    box. (*Puts a small tin money-box on table.*) You've got your
    small change out for cards. And remember I'm the referee,
    if I say it's swearing it is.
LEN: Already had this once today. I'm nearly fucking skint.
CHARLES: One.
LEN: Oh, fuck it.
CHARLES: Two.
    (LEN *puts two coins in box.*)
LEN: Deal the cards so we don't have to talk.
    (KEVIN *collects the pack.* ERIC *performs a strange movement: he
    shoots out one arm, displays wrist-watch, reaches into pocket
    and brings out cigarette case and lighter. He takes out an
    imaginary cigarette and lights it. Others watch.*)
CHARLES: What's that meant to be?
ERIC: What d'you *think*?
CHARLES: Some curious tropical variant of St Vitus' Dance?
ERIC: I'm working out a movement for when I'm back in
    Blighty, to display my Swiss watch, silver cigarette case
    and Ronson lighter all in one. I haven't yet included my
    Parker pen but all in good time . . .
CHARLES: I'd advise you against adding any other movement. It
    already looks like an epileptic seizure.

ERIC: Practice makes perfect, Squire. And when you imagine
   me in rimless specs and a Harris Tweed jacket——
CHARLES: I've seen the jacket. I've seen you trying it on in the
   basha.
KEVIN: We've all seen you. Sitting there in your Chinese Harris
   Tweed jacket drinking lemonade.
CHARLES: That's what aggravates your prickly heat.
ERIC: I happen to think a little discomfort is easily borne for the
   sake of cutting a dash.
LEN: You look like something the cat's dragged in.
ERIC: Laugh away. The day I walk up Susan's garden path
   we'll see who's laughing——
KEVIN: How much this Ronson lighter cost you?
ERIC: Ten chips. Which you'll agree is rock-bottom for a
   genuine English Ronson.
KEVIN: (*Looking at it carefully*) You read what it says on this
   genuine Ronson? 'Made in British.' (*He laughs.*)
CHARLES: Oh, no. Love, you've done it again. It's Hong Kong
   imitation.
ERIC: (*Looking at lighter*) Ruddy cheek! Well, anyway, they
   won't know the difference back home. I'll give it to Susan's
   Dad. Token of my esteem.
LEN: Here, look at that. All that fucking panic getting off I
   forgot this letter come for you this morning. That's your
   fiancée's handwriting, ain't it?
CHARLES: Swearword.
   (LEN *gives letter to* ERIC, *feeds coin into box.*)
ERIC: A New Malden postmark but it's not Susan's writing, no.
   Not her Dad's either.
   (*During the following* ERIC *opens and reads the letter.*)
LEN: What about dealing them sodding cards, Lambeth?
   (CHARLES *rattles box and* LEN *pays. And so on throughout
   scene.*)
KEVIN: (*Shuffling*) Eh, Brum, how d'you get in this skive in the
   first place?
LEN: What? Entertainments? Ain't I never told you?
KEVIN: Elocution, wasn't it? Shakespeare? Or was it to clean out
   the crapper? I forget.

LEN: (*As* KEVIN *pays*) I come in as an accordionist. Piano-fucking-accordionist. I used to be with Al Fresco and his Piano-accordion Hooligans.

KEVIN: Go on.

LEN: Straight up.

KEVIN: You ain't really played with them, have you?

LEN: Ain't I never showed you the picture?

KEVIN: Picture?

LEN: Photograph.

> (LEN *has been taking photo from wallet and now shows* KEVIN.)

There you are. Didn't fucking believe me, did you?

KEVIN: This is just you on your own in the back yard playing the accordion.

LEN: What d'you think it was going to be?

KEVIN: I thought it was going to be with Fresco's Accordion Hooligans.

LEN: I had to fucking practise, didn't I?

KEVIN: You aren't half a dopey sod. How d'you stand him, Charlotte?

CHARLES: I love him—so it's easy——

> (CHARLES *aware of* ERIC *staring at the letter*.)

What's the matter, is Susan all right? Who's the letter from?

ERIC: My mucker Roy Lawrence.

CHARLES: I remember. Billed himself as the Airman with the Flying Feet.

ERIC: I asked him to deliver the silk and lace for Susan's wedding dress.

CHARLES: Oh, yes. Did he manage it?

ERIC: (*Nods*) She's going to marry *him* instead. 'Neither of us meant this to happen but we couldn't help ourselves. It is hard to put into words but when you come home I will explain everything.' (*Puts down letter. Others silent.*) I'll say he'll ruddy well explain everything. At the double, before he gets a bunch of fives where it hurts him most.

CHARLES: Now, come on, Eric, take it easy——

ERIC: I'll soon have this lot sorted out, never fear. Who do they think they are, what? Damned cheek! Couldn't help

87

themselves? Why not, would you mind telling me?

(ERIC *looks at the others as though expecting an answer. Train sounds continue.*)

KEVIN: Looks to me as though he's helped himself to quite a tidy slice.

(ERIC *takes off glasses and polishes with handkerchief.*)

ERIC: Here have I been keeping myself for her and all of a sudden, out of the blue, I get a mess-pot. And she doesn't even send it, she gets *him* to send it. She and I used to do our prep together . . . we were tennis partners . . . she assisted with the magic . . . and now she can turn me down for . . . he never even went to a decent grammar school, just some wretched elementary . . . (*Stops, bites lip, stands and makes to go.*)

CHARLES: Shall I make you some lemonade? You brought a tin of crystals?

(ERIC *stands, makes to go, bumps into door, searches for glasses.* LEN *gives them to him.* ERIC *goes, taking letter. Silence for a moment, but for the train wheels.*)

LEN: Women? A load of cunts. (*Puts coin in tin.*)

(CHARLES *puts his hand on* LEN's, *raises it to his lips and kisses it.*)

(*More place signs brought on by Chinese and* REG: *Seremban, Kajang, Kuala Lumpur.*)

(*Train music and the line pistons across again, drawing off the compartment with steam and whistles. The music slows down to a halt.* TERRI *in spot. Cloth down.*)

TERRI: I wasn't sorry to be leaving the island, I don't mind telling you. There'd been a constant to-and-fro of the China Fleet across my balcony—ships that pass in the night. One of my ratings had been glimpsed wrestling with the trellis on his way home and eyebrows were being raised over the pink gins at Raffles. Now I'd already been tersely turned off Malta on the way East. 'This is an outrage,' I kept shouting on the jetty, 'I have no political convictions.' But sauce only gets you so far and I was glad to be moving out of danger into something a bit more peaceful.

GILES: (*Other side*) From Kuala Lumpur we went by road—a

couple of jeeps, a fifteen hundredweight and a three-ton gharry. At the rear armed sentries, tail-boards down for a quick getaway in case of ambush. Bren guns loaded with actions cocked, mounted on the driver's cabin raking the road ahead. I felt a familiar but almost-forgotten tightening of the stomach. Years of boredom fell away, like an old skin. Now that our lives were in danger, they suddenly became infinitely precious. I prayed for our safety and thanked Almighty God that at last the *real* show had begun.

SCENE SIX
Highland Games

Chinese percussion as cloth flies revealing a divan bed centre. There is an open suitcase on it. A tartan backcloth closes off a small acting area.
Flickering firelight from downstage completes the impression of a cold night in the hills. Percussion stops. REG *brings on one more place-name: The Cameron Highlands. Goes.*
Knock on door. SYLVIA *comes on wearing cardigan, woollen skirt, etc.*

SYLVIA: Come in!
    (STEVE *enters, far side, with army jumper over KD.*)
    Hullo, Stranger.
STEVE: You've got a nice room.
SYLVIA: Come and sit by the fire.
    (STEVE *comes towards* SYLVIA, *looking at fire, holds out and warms his hands.*)
STEVE: I can't get over the cold.
SYLVIA: I told you I'd dress like an English girl for you, don't you remember? Look: a lambswool cardigan. And stockings. (*She lifts her skirt, showing her stocking-tops. He looks at the fire. Silence.*) Listen, Steve, tell me if I'm being silly, I have the distinct impression you've been avoiding me.
STEVE: What makes you think that?

89

SYLVIA: Is it true?

STEVE: The old man seems to have picked on me as a substitute son. I hardly get a moment to myself. He's decided I'm officer material.

SYLVIA: D'you think you are?

STEVE: Of course not.

SYLVIA: Tell him then.

STEVE: He's not much of a listener. He doesn't really hear.

SYLVIA: I always think he's a typical Englishman. Kind-hearted, shy, intelligent——

STEVE: He hasn't a clue how the rest of us live. He thinks we still say 'law, love a duck' and 'stone the crows'.

SYLVIA: As long as that's the only reason you haven't been seeing me. It did occur to me that you were staying away because I'm pregnant.

STEVE: Why should I stay away for that?

SYLVIA: (*Shrugs*) You knew so little about how a baby is conceived and born . . . I mean, you do appreciate, don't you, that because a girl's expecting doesn't mean she can't go to bed with her boy. In fact, they can go on doing jig-jig right up to the last weeks, if they want to—great heavens above, what are you laughing at now?

STEVE: That word: jig-jig. It's a tart's word. And a pimp's word. Those old stagecoaches in Calcutta with little girls' faces peering out: 'You want jig-jig, sahib? Me? My sister? Clean girl, working way through college? You want jig-jig my mother? My little brother?'

SYLVIA: Making fun of my Welsh accent again.

STEVE: I was making fun of the word jig-jig. I was wondering what they'd make of it in Fernleaze Crescent, Swindon.

SYLVIA: Good grief, I shan't say it to your mother. If I'd said it to my mother, she'd have slapped my face. You think I don't know how to behave? I suppose you're afraid one day you and your mother and I will be strolling round Harrods and I shall say something to let you down?

STEVE: My Mum's never *heard* of Harrods. *I'd* never heard of it till you told me. I asked Major Flack and he said yes that's right——

SYLVIA: Don't you trust a word I say?

STEVE: —It's a big shop for the middle and upper classes. Well, my mum used to say *we* were middle class but I see now we were actually *lower* middle, one cut above working.

SYLVIA: I notice you managed to make him listen to *some* things.

STEVE: *Most* English people have never heard of Harrods. Typical Englishmen, that is. Not him, the top two or three per cent, but the rest of us.

SYLVIA: You can buy enormous beds there. Four-posters. And they will deliver prams and toys within a radius of fifty miles.

(STEVE *goes on staring into the fire.*)

Come and sit here.

STEVE: I'm just getting warm.

SYLVIA: We'll make it warm in bed, shall we? We'll warm those freezing sheets.

STEVE: I can't stay that long. The old man expects me. We're reading *Pilgrim's Progress*.

SYLVIA: Didn't you ask him about my passage home? Or whether he'd be our best man?

(STEVE *sits on bed.* SYLVIA *touches him.*)

The nicest thing about being pregnant, darling, is that there's absolutely no danger of *getting* pregnant.

STEVE: Will you listen a minute? I was going to write you a letter but . . . that would have been easier but not fair to you . . . you know today was pay-day? Look—— (*He takes out wad of banknotes.*)

Here's my back pay for my extra stripes from the day Reg got killed. I've talked to one or two people who've been around a bit and they say that would be enough for a decent operation. I wouldn't let you go in for anything risky or sordid but a proper nursing home—well, you'd obviously know more about that than—I don't mean you especially, of course, but any woman would . . . hardly fail to know more than me. (*Rises and moves. Pause.*) More than *I* would.

SYLVIA: You don't want me to have the baby?

STEVE: It's not a question of what I want. They're not ready for it in Fernleaze Crescent.

SYLVIA: But we'll be married, everything will be completely respectable.

STEVE: They're not ready for *any* of it. Even if I married the girl next door, they'd think I was too young. Dad's quite broad-minded but Mum thinks I'm still a child. She last saw me at eighteen. If I come home with a foreign wife . . .
(*He shakes his head hopelessly. Pause.* SYLVIA *stares.*)
God, society's such a mess . . . (*Another pause. He looks at her.*)

SYLVIA: I knew this was coming but to be quite honest I'm almost paralysed, to tell you the exact truth. I do respect you for speaking frankly, that's really important in a case like this, I agree entirely. All the same it's a shock to know for certain because you were the first man I really loved——

STEVE: Oh, come on, Sylvia——

SYLVIA: Oh, yes, it was love at first sight. But then being with you such a long time my love became deeper. Your personality, your determined character . . . and then when you were kissing my body or making love, it was just the most wonderful experience . . . come and sit by me here.

STEVE: We mustn't be weak about this.

SYLVIA: Just hold my hand a minute.
(*He does.*)
Don't you appreciate anything else about me but the jig—sleeping together? I don't mean love even, I mean simply being a friend. A friend that you like to go to bed with, wouldn't that be rather nice?

STEVE: It's not a question of what's nice or what *we* want but society! And until we can change society, how can we change ourselves? And that means changing every person *in* society, so there'll be no more wars or colonies or race prejudice.
(SYLVIA *stares at* STEVE. *He looks at his watch, gets up.*)
The old man's expecting me. We must talk about this properly some time. Really talk out all the issues thoroughly.
(STEVE *goes.* SYLVIA *buries her face in the bed.*)

(*Music of next number and the prompters and* REG *bring on more place-name placards: Kuala Kangar, Sungei Siput, Kampong Malang . . .*)
(*The front-cloth drops and a spot finds* KEVIN.)

SCENE SEVEN
Si, Si, Si

KEVIN: (*Sings*) Flashing eyes, scarlet lips,
Talking fingers, swaying hips,
Fruity hats, cool verandah,
No one else but La Miranda!

(ERIC *and* LEN *in frilly shirts come on playing guitars, maracas, etc.* TERRI *follows, as described. The trio accompanies his song.*)

TERRI: Have you ever been-a
Down in Argentina,
Have you ever known zat special thrill?
How d'you like to mail-a
Card from Venezuela?
You could find romance in old Brazil.
And in Valparaiso
Girls would roll their eyes-so
That you could not tear yourself away.
Come and have a gala
Down in Guatemala,
The Latin-American Way.

Come and spend a week-a
Down in Costa Rica,
Come and lose your heart in Vera Cruz.
Easy to catch a barracuda
Right by your hotel in Bermuda,
That's the way we chase away the blues.
Think how you could brag you are

Weekending in Nicaragua
Or wearing funny hats in Uruguay.
Kill a nice vicuña
Underneath the moon-a,
The Latin-American Way.

Every senorita
Welcome in the fleet-a
And she pray her favourite saint to bless.
Guys who rock the boat-a
They won't get my vote-a,
I prefer American Express.
Down in old Havana
Life is all mañana,
No one work and everybody play.
How could you resist a
Weekend with Batista,
The Latin-American Way?
(*Music reprise and they all samba off, as cloth is flown.*)

SCENE EIGHT
The North of Gongapooch

Hangings or screens represent an improvised dressing-room. A fold-up table and chairs either side with make-up, etc, single overhead light bulb, clothes on rack. Hear the concert party performing offstage. CHARLES *is finishing his face in a hand-mirror.* TERRI *enters as Miranda, tearing off headdress.*

TERRI: Well, I've played some number three touring-dates in my time but never anything to touch Kampong Uvula.
CHARLES: I don't remember coming here with Tropic Scandals.
(TERRI *turns back to* CHARLES, *who unzips his dress. Through scene* TERRI *gets out of drag.*)
TERRI: Terri Dennis thanks Gillian Flack for a most enjoyable engagement at His Majesty's, Tampon Kotex, with many

94

happy memories of the star dressing-room.

CHARLES: And the lovely audiences.

TERRI: Don't! Not a single white face, just row upon row of brave little Gurkhas. It's like staring at a pound of prunes.

CHARLES: They say they never take out their kukris without drawing blood.

TERRI: I've always wanted to put that to the test.

CHARLES: Oh, dear. Another double-entendre.

TERRI: Hello.

CHARLES: Well, there's nothing very funny about Gurkhas, is there? A race of mercenary savages who'll fight for the British against their fellow-Asians.

TERRI: My dear, is it your time of the month?

CHARLES: Don't you ever tire of changing he to she or calling men by women's names? There's nothing funny about being like this, either.

TERRI: Like what? Gay, you mean?

CHARLES: Queer. What's gay about it? Most men like women and most women like men. We're *queer*, Terri, queer as coots. And I don't think we should flaunt this cruel trick of nature. I think we should behave ourselves *more* than normal people. Your kind of promiscuity goes too far. At your age you should be settling down. There.

(*Pause.* TERRI *takes off dress and hangs it on rack, he lights a cigarette, sits facing* CHARLES.)

TERRI: And of course you're safe in the arms of Jessica.

CHARLES: Sorry. Did it sound like that? My Salvationist background.

TERRI: You're safe for the time being but sooner or later you'll be on the boat, leaving hubby on the Equator. England, 1948, is a far cry from the Fleet Club, duckie. One lonely night you'll say a few flattering words to some nice chap in a cottage and next you know a cow of a magistrate's giving you three months.

CHARLES: I'm not going home. I'm signing on to stay with Len. We've sworn to stay with each other, whatever happens.

TERRI: Not going on the stage then?

CHARLES: Well, tell me honestly, d'you think I've got a chance?

95

(CHARLES *moves to the rack and takes down a furry overcoat.*
TERRI *examines his face in the glass.*)

TERRI: One must have talent or looks or preferably both. I was
never Nijinsky, but I was a pretty face.

CHARLES: And I'm not?

TERRI: The head in the middle's not bad.

CHARLES: Thank you. So I suspected. (*Putting on coat.*) And as
I'm no ornament I might as well be useful. I'm going back
to male nursing.

TERRI: What about Len's wife?

CHARLES: She's not bothered, there's plenty of what she wants
at Aldershot.

TERRI: Len's a lucky man.

CHARLES: I'm lucky too.

STEVE: (*Entering*) Come on, Charles, you're nearly on.

TERRI: Thank your lucky stars you didn't fall for our
sergeant major.

STEVE: Kevin's number's just finishing.

TERRI: He'd have put you in the family way and left you for
some suck-off antics with the Major.

CHARLES: Any British turned up yet?

STEVE: Still out on patrol. Now get on.

(CHARLES *goes.* STEVE *makes to follow.*)

At the double!

TERRI: Wouldn't you? Duckie?

STEVE: (*Almost pleading*) I'm trying to do my best by everyone!

(STEVE *follows* CHARLES *off.* TERRI *shakes head sadly.*)

(*Cloth comes down.*)

SCENE NINE
Pals

CHARLES *and* LEN *stroll on crooning a Flanagan-and-Allen kind of
song.* LEN *wears suit and* CHARLES *fur coat and battered straw hat.*

CHARLES & LEN:	Though we've been far from Sunnyside Lane
	You've never heard us complain
	But now that we're due in out of the rain
	We'll never leave it again.
	And once we've left those cloudy skies
	You'll hear us saying, 'Howdy, guys';
	Once Mister Blues is on the run,
	You'll hear us greeting Mister Sun.

CHORUS:	Oh, we've been content
	Though we've never had a cent
	Because I've had you and you've had me,
	And every trouble and care
	Seemed so much less hard to bear
	'Cos we bore them in each other's company.

Through all the stormclouds we've been true
To one another, just we two,
But now the rainbow's in the blue,
The sun will soon be shining through.
And though we've too often strayed
From the bright side to the shade,
Together we shall never more roam
From the heart of home sweet home.

(*Exeunt.*)
(*Front-cloth goes up on full stage, empty, but bordered by dim jungle cut-outs. Bleak front lighting.*)

SCENE TEN
Even Their Relations Think They're Funny

TERRI *enters in light suit as compère.*

TERRI: Thank you so much. So now you've seen a little of Costa Rica, we've brought you the heart-aches and joys of an Atlantic convoy and we've heard from one of the girls who's waiting for you at home. Well, not *you*, perhaps—anyway

97

now Deception with a Difference brought to you by Love the Magician. Or for those of you who speak Spanish. El Amor Brujo. Not a titter. As a matter of interest, how many of you even speak English? Even *understand* English?

GILES: (*From audience*) I speak English.

TERRI: Well, screw *you* for a start.

GILES: Please watch your language, Mr Dennis——

TERRI: Oh, you! Then you're the only one who's got the faintest idea what we're on about. No wonder it's so quiet.

GILES: They're enjoying it in their own way. They'll understand the conjuring. Carry on!

TERRI: Here she is then—Mean, Moody, Magnificent—Young-Love!

(ERIC *comes on wearing flowing gown, smoking cigarette. Stares at* TERRI *angrily but* TERRI *goes.* ERIC *does some passes, makes cigarette vanish, reappear, etc.*)

ERIC: The last time I did this trick was at Raffles Hotel, Singapore. I think. (*Takes silver spoon from pocket, looks at it.*) Yes, Raffles Hotel. As a matter of fact, this isn't my usual line at all. I'm an operatic tenor. I was trained abroad. All the neighbours made a collection. My favourite song is the Milkmaid's Song: We must all pull together.

GILES: Too much talk. Get on with it, man.

ERIC: Sir!

(SYLVIA *enters in long dress, bringing table and props.* ERIC *takes cards, shuffles, squirts them into top hat held by* SYLVIA.)

This is known as the Russian Shuffle. Because, as you see, the cards are Russian from one end to the other.

(SYLVIA *puts hat on table.* ERIC *produces flowers from cloak. She shows empty cylinder to audience.*)

Sylvia, my assistant, is showing you that there is nothing in the cylinder.

(ERIC *takes it from* SYLVIA *and waves with magic wand.*)

Completely empty. It's rather like a girl on a windy day. Now you see it, now you don't.

GILES: No smut, thank you.

ERIC: No, sir. I give it two taps with the magic wand. Two taps

—one hot, one cold—and hey presto——

(*The lights go out.*)

Ah, now there appears to be a slight technical hitch.

GILES: Carry on, I'll soon have it mended.

ERIC: Hey presto, voilà! I should perhaps explain that at this moment I am producing a variety of coloured handkerchiefs from the apparently empty cylinder.

(*Pause.*)

SYLVIA: The last time I did——

ERIC: The last time I did this trick I had the audience in the palm of my hand. Which will give you some idea of the size of the audience.

(*Shriek of an animal in the jungle.*)

Observe also that during this trick my hand never leaves the end of my arm. And there they are, all tied together. Thank you. And now my assistant is going to come down amongst you for a volunteer——

SYLVIA: Don't be absurd, Eric! I wouldn't go near those fellows in the dark.

TERRI: Pack it in, love. I'll get the pianist to play something——

(*Lights on.* ERIC *is falling with the table. Props everywhere.* SYLVIA *and others help him clear them up.* TERRI *comes down.*)

And now may I have your attention for something a shade more serious?

(*The animal shrieks again.*)

Thank you, Ada. A dramatic recitation.

   'By the old Moulmein Pagoda looking eastward to the sea
   There's a Burma girl a-waiting and I know she thinks of me;
   For the wind is in the palm-trees and the temple-bells——'

KEVIN: (*Entering*) Excuse me.

TERRI: What? I'm trying to recite.

KEVIN: I've got an urgent police message.

TERRI: An urgent police message? Then read it this instant.

KEVIN: (*Reading note*) Will the person known as Pharaoh last heard of two thousand years ago in Egypt, please go to the British Museum where his mummy's lying dangerously ill.

TERRI: Will you please get off the stage and permit me to

continue. 'For the wind is in the palm-trees——'
(STEVE *comes on with a bucket.*)
Where are you off to?

STEVE: To see my brother.

TERRI: Where is he?

STEVE: He's in jail.

TERRI: What's the bucket for?

STEVE: To bail him out.

TERRI: I'm trying to give these little brown gentlemen a
recitation. 'Come you back, you British soldier, come you
back to Mandalay——'
(LEN *returns with bucket, wearing crinoline and wig.*)
Where are you going?

LEN: To milk a cow.

TERRI: In that wig?

LEN: No, in this bucket. (*Goes off, spilling water from bucket.*)

TERRI: Kindly leave the upturned tea-chests. 'For the wind is in
the palm-trees and the temple bells they say——'
(KEVIN *returns with bucket, throws at audience, only confetti.*)
(CHARLES *comes on as* KEVIN *goes off.*)
'And the temple bells they say——'

CHARLES: Excuse me——

TERRI: Excuse me, British soldier—no! D'you mind? I'm trying
to recite poetry.

CHARLES: Poetry? Ah, poetry! 'The dog stood on the burning
deck, The flames were leaping round his neck——
Hot dog!'

TERRI: (*Desperate*) 'Come you back, you British soldier——'

KEVIN: (*Entering*) Where's the Major?

TERRI: Where's the Major? I don't know, where *is*——

KEVIN: They're attacking the camp——

TERRI: I'm attempting to recite Kipling——

KEVIN: They're inside, I've seen them——

TERRI: I don't remember this, duckie, what's the——
(LEN *runs on, wearing crinoline.*)

LEN: They've knifed the fucking guard, the fucking commies.
(LEN *turns to shout at audience as* LEE *and* CHENG *come on
upstage with stens.*)

Bandit shoot Gurkha chowkidar——

(*Lights go out and in the darkness* LEE *and* CHENG *fire rapid bursts towards audience. Cries of alarm and pain from everyone onstage.*)

(*Lights come on again and* REG *enters upstage, also with sten.*)

REG: I said girl and sergeant major.

(*The others have fallen on to the stage.* REG *goes to stand over* LEN.)

This no girl. This Blitish corporal. Come, looksee, upside downside——

(REG *goes off with* LEE *and* CHENG *as* SYLVIA *comes from hiding behind a wardrobe skip, staring after* REG. STEVE *comes from other side and they seize each other. They look at the wounded lying around them.*)

(GILES *comes on downstage and speaks to* FOH.)

GILES: Right. Thank you.

(*Lights down again on the carnage and a spot on* GILES.)

I sensed this might be an ambush when we arrived and found all the British were out on patrol. I was on the alert from the word go. The first sign of danger was when the lights went out. I made straight for our generator and sure enough found the juice had been switched off so after turning it on again I began inspecting the immediate vicinity. Thus it chanced that when the shooting began I was not actually on the spot. The bandits killed two guards and helped themselves to all the arms they could lay hands on but it seemed to me an immensely foolhardy operation. In the ordinary way, of course, Lights Out would have been at sundown and all the Gurkhas would have been asleep. Imagine the terrorists' consternation, then, at being faced with row upon row of unsmiling Mongol faces watching a British comedy show. This was indeed a Jungle Jamboree they had not anticipated. At any rate they panicked and let off bursts of rapid fire into the midst of them. Now that was very bad thinking because Johnny Gurkha doesn't stand arguing the toss, it's out with his kukri and off with their heads. Four of the Chinamen were taken before I could reach them and I'm afraid were hideously mutilated. Two more we took prisoner and any others sneaked off into the jungle leaving their comrades to face the music. The terrorists got a total bag of four: three Gurkhas and one BOR. Making a final score of six-four to us.

(*Lights behind show various casualties lying about in tableau, attended or mourned by the others.* LEN *is particularly clear, lying on his own while* CHARLES *bandages* TERRI's *leg.* SYLVIA *and* STEVE *nurse* KEVIN *and* ERIC *moves about with buckets.* GILES *does not acknowledge this.*)

I was sorry to lose poor Bonny. He was one of the best. Not perhaps bursting with imagination but steady, loyal, dependable. After being brought up in the sewers of Birmingham, the darkness and filth of the jungle held no terrors for him. And if you'd praised him for playing his part in the defence of freedom, he might well have protested 'Lor' bless my soul, sir, that's a load of 'umbug and no error . . .'

(CHARLES *comes down to* LEN *and kneels beside him.*)

A particularly tragic aspect of his death is that I'd recently arranged—without his knowledge—to have his wife posted out to join him. This was to have been a pleasant surprise on our return to Singapore.

(CHARLES *kisses* LEN's *face.*)

Alas, this happy reunion was not to be. And as he went he said, 'Death, where is thy sting?' And as he went down deeper he said, 'Grave, where is thy victory?' So he passed over and all the trumpets sounded for him on the other side.

SCENE ELEVEN
Finale: Bless 'em All

Lights go down on tableau and up on front-cloth as GILES *exits.*

SPEAKER: Attention, please, attention, please. Civilians, officers and British other ranks are now boarding SS *Albion*. Homeward bound personnel will assemble immediately for embarkation of Godown 42. Sub-cheese luggage-wallahs aboard karo ekdum.

(*The front-cloth represents a dock scene: sheds, piles of cargo, cranes above, signs on wall pointing 'East' and 'West'. Bright light.* CHARLES *enters pushing* KEVIN *in a wheelchair.*)

KEVIN: There she is, Charlie. The boat. We made it.

(CHARLES *stops and brakes the chair facing one side. The gangplank comes down and rests at an angle to represent the way on board.*)

CHARLES: Some of us.

KEVIN: After a fashion.

CHARLES: There is some fucking corner of a foreign fucking field that is forever fucking England.

KEVIN: I'm glad to see it, all the same. Glad to be going home and all, even though I'll never know what it's like to have a white bint. I mean, it was all in a good cause. We kept the old flag flying, eh? Helped save a bit of the Empire from the Chinese, eh?

CHARLES: Having brought them here in the first place to work our tin mines.

KEVIN: We may be a tiny little island, Charlie, but no one pushes us about.

CHARLES: My dear, keeping rubber for democracy won't give you back your balls. Or Len his life. What odds would it make to Len whether England was Communist, Fascist or Anabaptist? He'd still be working in a stores somewhere, making lists, getting what he could out of life . . .

KEVIN: I reckon if he could speak to us now——

CHARLES: He can't though, can he? He never could. Born in a dump in Smethwick that's not one of the things you learn.

(ERIC *comes, same way, carrying kit-bag, which he dumps upstage.*)

ERIC: Come along then, juldi, juldi, what are we waiting for?

KEVIN: The Old Man. We've all got to assemble on the dock, he wants to say a few words.

CHARLES: Tell me when he doesn't.

ERIC: Sooner we get mobile sooner I'll be home to sort out creepie-crawlie Roy Lawrence of the Flying Feet. He'll dance to another tune, believe me.

(ERIC *shoots out wrist to look at watch, takes out cigarette case, gives* KEVIN *one and takes one himself.*)

CHARLES: What good's a bunch of fives going to do? They're engaged.

ERIC: Then they can ruddy well get disengaged, my old mucker. At the double!

CHARLES: Face facts——

ERIC: Facts? The facts are Susan's my girl and he's pushed in. The facts are—— (*He has been trying to work his lighter but now gives up.*) I hope this is the last I see of damned cheapjack Chinese rubbish!

(KEVIN *supplies a match as* STEVE *and* SYLVIA *are driven on in trishaw by* LEE. *She is beginning to show her pregnancy and is prettily dressed as for a garden party;* STEVE *is uniformed. But has one arm in sling and splint.*)

SYLVIA: Hallo, boys, better late than never!

STEVE: Where's the old man?

KEVIN: No sign yet.

(STEVE *helps* SYLVIA *down.* LEE *begins unloading her hand baggage for the voyage.* STEVE *comes to audience.*)

STEVE: Dear everyone at 56, this is the last you'll hear before the boat. Five weeks' time I'll be with you all, by which time my arm should be almost mended.

(*The other men help* LEE *and talk to* SYLVIA.)

Thank you for getting my old room ready but can you fit in a *double*-bed because my wife Sylvia will be coming with me! She is half-Indian, half-Welsh and I'm quite sure you will all make her feel at home because she is so looking forward to meeting you and her grandma who lives in Swansea.

SYLVIA: (*Who's joined* STEVE) Don't forget to tell them I'm pregnant.

STEVE: And here's another surprise: within a few months you'll be grandparents and Graham will become an uncle. Sorry not to have told you sooner but with all that trouble in the jungle it slipped my mind. So you see, Dad, the army *has* made a man of me, though rather late in the day. See you soon, don't write any more——

SYLVIA: Sylvia sends her love——

STEVE: And so do I. Steve.

(STEVE *and* SYLVIA *go upstage and* STEVE *pays* LEE, *who drives off.* SYLVIA *looks about anxiously. Meanwhile:*)

SPEAKER: Attention, please, attention, please. All British other ranks are now embarking at Godown 42. Hurry it up there. (*Ship's horn sounded.*)

STEVE: Young-Love, you're in trouble——

ERIC: How's that, Chiefy?

STEVE: See that redcap at the entrance to the wharf?

ERIC: Yes.

STEVE: Don't let *him* see *you.*

ERIC: Why not?

STEVE: He's out to arrest you.

ERIC: Me? What for? My nose is clean.

STEVE: They want you for receiving stolen goods. Two Irish cooks are being court-martialled for illegally disposing of tins of lemonade powder.

ERIC: I didn't know they'd *stolen* it. They told me it was gash. I'm on the boat, my number's up, they can't do this to me!

STEVE: They won't if you keep out of the MP's way. I told him you haven't come on yet. He's waiting there to catch you.

ERIC: Thank you, Chief, I shan't forget this. I'll see you all right on the boat. Anything you want, Squire, just say the word. How about a genuine English Ronson?

CHARLES: Calm down, your prickly heat will be flaring up again . . . (ERIC *hides behind others during rest of scene.*)

SYLVIA: Where's the Major got to?

STEVE: You stop panicking too.

SYLVIA: I'm like a cat on hot bricks. I keep expecting to see Reg Drummond.

STEVE: That Gurkha got him, I tell you. Just as *he* was about to get me. I saw the kukri——

SYLVIA: You didn't see him fall. Nearly thirty years I've waited for this day, for this very moment. But Mummy always said: there's many a slip twixt the cup and the lip. And no one knew better than she!

STEVE: You native women are all the same: riddled with superstition.

(STEVE *kisses* SYLVIA *as* TERRI *enters, walking with sticks to support an injured leg. With him is* CHENG *in uniform of Civil Police, carrying a suitcase, which he puts down.*)

TERRI: This is an outrage! I've never been so insulted throughout the whole of my professional career!

CHARLES: Not another drama?

TERRI: Drama! I've given my all for the boys and my reward is being rushed to the boat as though I'd got the Black Death. I keep telling this officer I have no political convictions but look at her! The Laughing Policewoman!

SYLVIA: You've been misbehaving again.

TERRI: Talk about the pottle calling the kettle. My dear!

STEVE: What happened?

TERRI: I got discharged from hospital yesterday and spent the day quietly with friends. Late at night I arrived back at Raffles with this sweet little matelot, hobbled up to my room and let him in without switching on the lights. He was all over me before I could draw breath. 'Ooo, sir, you're a smasher, ooo, sir, you're a dream!' I asked him could he possibly forget I was an officer for the time being but it's strange how many of them like all that, the suck-off antics, so I let him rave on—'Oh, Captain, let me give you a baby' until he had to run and catch the liberty boat. I waved goodbye from the balcony and was back in the room lighting a soothing Churchman's when suddenly a voice said 'Could you please oblige me with a match?'

SYLVIA: Oh, Terri! Where from?

TERRI: The other bed. There'd always been two and in my absence they'd filled the other. With the mosquito net pulled down, I hadn't noticed Ada.

CHARLES: Who was it?

TERRI: Some old duck.

SYLVIA: What did he say?

TERRI: That was the last I heard till morning when the manager told me I'd be escorted to the docks and put on the next boat home.

CHARLES: So the man in the bed had shopped you?

TERRI: There's some would sell their mother for a cream slice.

KEVIN: But you were going on this boat anyway.

TERRI: That's not the point. Is this the way to treat a celebrated war heroine? One who's made the sacrifices I've made. (*Rounds on* CHENG.) I shan't let it rest, believe me. You'll be hearing from my member.

SPEAKER: All visitors ashore now, please, all visitors ashore. Sub-cheese coolies ashore karo juldi-juldi.

(*Ship's siren.*)

ERIC: Let's get on board, Chief, this pier's crawling with rozzers.

SYLVIA: Oh, yes, darling, please, let's not miss the boat after all this time.

STEVE: All right, everyone, you get on board, I'll wait for the Old Man——

(GILES *comes on from side, with* LEE *now as coolie carrying his personal luggage.*)

GILES: (*Saluting*) Stand easy. Well, everyone, we shall certainly meet again during the five weeks at sea but as fellow-passengers, not comrades-in-arms. So I want to take this last opportunity of inviting you to drop in for tea if you find yourself in Berkshire. Nothing remarkable, of course, only a simple seventeenth-century mill-house, typical of hundreds throughout the length and breadth of England. No very brilliant company either—only my wife and the Labradors.

(GILES *addresses much of this to* STEVE.)

Perhaps a spot of hunting, freshwater fishing. If any of you is a rubber, there's a fine Jacobean brass in the Norman church. In other words, the ordinary everyday England we've been serving to save. Worth fighting for, worth dying for. There can be no peace without war, no war without sacrifice. Many more lives and limbs will be lost in South East Asia before freedom is safe and the survivors may go home to enjoy the precious fruits of freedom. For whether he chooses a humble cottage, a great house or only a bamboo hovel in a jungle clearing, every soldier dreams of the day when he can say—as we say now——

(GILES *leads them into a reprise of the Home-Sweet-Home song.*)

ALL: We're going back
To that homely little shack
On the sunny side of Any Street.
We've been too long
From the laughter and the song
That we'll share with all the folks we're going to meet.

I know a lady living there
With shining eyes and silver hair
And when she offers me a chair
I'm going to feel a millionaire.

So though we've travelled around
Now's the time to settle down
And when we're there we'll never more roam
From the heart of home-sweet-home.

(*Meanwhile the cloth goes up revealing more dockside with a gangplank at stage floor leading offstage at an angle.* LEE *goes aboard with Giles's luggage. After the first reprise of the song* GILES *shakes hands with the company while the music continues.* LEE *returns empty-handed and* GILES *gives him money.*)

SYLVIA: (*Apart*) Oh, good grief, what a slowcoach! I shan't feel completely safe until we're on that boat and they've pulled up the plank.

STEVE: Superstition! Eastern superstition. Who are you scared of?

SYLVIA: Reg. I've got a feeling he'll always be with us. In some form or another.

STEVE: We'll keep our eyes open.

(CHENG *blows his police whistle and the line reforms as they follow* GILES *towards the gangplank in this order:* STEVE, SYLVIA, ERIC, KEVIN *wheeled by* CHARLES, *and* TERRI.)

ALL: So though we've travelled around
Now it's time to settle down
And when we're there we'll never more stray

From the paradise that's sunny all day,
Which is why we're sailing over the foam
To the heart of home-sweet-home.
(*And as they move across, we see that* REG *is on the end of the line, dressed Chinese. He puts his finger to his lips, instructing silence, singing. The men wave to us,* LEE *and* CHENG *remain on stage level waving at them.*)